W9-AQT-621

THE SUBJECT MATTERS

THE SUBJECT MATTERS

Classroom Activity in Math and Social Studies

SUSAN S. STODOLSKY

CARNEGIE LIBRARY
LIVINGSTONE COLLEGE
SALISBURY, NC 28144

THE UNIVERSITY OF CHICAGO PRESS

Chicago and London

122679

Susan S. Stodolsky is associate professor of education and the behavioral
sciences at the University of Chicago.

The University of Chicago Press, Chicago 60637
The University of Chicago Press, Ltd., London
© 1988 by The University of Chicago
All rights reserved. Published 1988
Printed in the United States of America
97 96 95 94 93 92 91 90 89 88   5 4 3 2 1

LIBRARY OF CONGRESS CATALOGING-IN-PUBLICATION DATA
Stodolsky, Susan S.
   The subject matters: classroom activity in math and social
studies / Susan S. Stodolsky.
      p.   cm.
   Bibliography: p.
   Includes index.
   ISBN 0-226-77511-9
   1. Teaching—Case studies. 2. Activity programs in education—Case studies.
3. Mathematics—Study and teaching (Elementary)—Case studies. 4. Social
sciences—Study and teaching (Elementary)—Case studies. I. Title.
LB1027.25.S76   1988
372.11—dc19   87—23166
                                                                   CIP

TO MY MOTHER, RUTH P. SILVERMAN
AND THE MEMORY OF MY FATHER,
ABNER H. SILVERMAN

Contents

LIST OF TABLES   xi

LIST OF FIGURES   xiii

PREFACE   xv

1. SUBJECT MATTER, CLASSROOM
   ACTIVITY, AND STUDENT
   INVOLVEMENT   1
   Introduction   1
   Subject Matter and Instruction   3
     Mathematics Programs   7
     Social Studies Programs   8
   The Activity Structure and Activity Segments   11
     Segment Properties   12
   Student Involvement   15
     Background on Student Involvement   16

2. RESEARCH METHODS   20
   Selection of Schools, Classrooms, and Students   20
   Data Collection Procedures   22
     *Observations of Classroom Activity and
        Students   22*
   Data-Coding Procedures   26
     Identifying Segments   26
     Coding Segment Properties   26
     Coding Student Involvement   28
   Data Analysis   28
     Interdependence in the Data   28
   Basic Descriptive Information on the Observational
        Data   28

3. SUBJECT MATTER DIFFERENCES IN
CLASSROOM ACTIVITY   31
Lesson Topics   31
Instructional Activity   35
   Segment Feature Measures   40
   Instructional Formats   41
   Student Behavior Patterns   44
   Materials   48
   Pacing and Expected Social Interaction   49
   Options   56
   Location and Time of Day   57
   Feedback   58
   Cognitive Level   58
   Teacher Role and Simultaneous Segments   61
Segment Patterns   62
Program Variants   66
Individual Teachers   70
Summary   73

4. BEYOND SUBJECT MATTER:
INTELLECTUAL ACTIVITY AND
STUDENT RESPONSE   75
How Learning Environments Are Organized   76
   Cognitive Level and Pacing   78
Student Involvement   82
   *Cognitive Level, Pacing, and Student
      Involvement   83*
   Factual Teacher-Paced Segments   87
   Preparatory Segments   89
   Checking-Work Segments   90
   Recitation Segments   91
Discussion   93
   The Responsive Student   94
   Intellectual Activity   97

5. DISCUSSION AND IMPLICATIONS   103
Generalizability   104
Origins of Different Activity Structures   105
   Community Influences   105
   Students   107
   Tests—Accountability   108

Textbooks   110
Teachers   113
Content and Topics   115
The Meaning of Learning   117
Routes to Learning   121
Student Attitudes   126
Implications and Reflections   129
*The Existential Fallacy and Educational
    Research   129*
Implications   131

APPENDIX A. SAMPLE INSTRUMENTS   137
Activity Structure Observation Form   138
Individual Student Observation Form   141

APPENDIX B. CODING DEFINITIONS AND
EXAMPLES   142
Instructional Format   142
Pacing   147
Cognitive Level   148
Student Behavior   153
Teacher Leadership Role   158
Feedback   159
Expected Student Interaction   165
Task Options   166
Options When Done   167
Student Location   167
Student Involvement   168

APPENDIX C. TABLES   169
Table C.1 Number of Instructional Segments,
    Involvement Segments, Minutes, and Class
    Periods Observed in Each Class   170
Table C.2 Mean Durations of Segments by Segment
    Features   171

NOTES   175

REFERENCES   181

INDEX   191

List of Tables

2.1   Sample Characteristics   21

2.2   Teacher Designation and Characteristics of
Sample Classrooms   29

3.1   Distributions of Instructional Formats   43

3.2   Distributions of Student Behavior Patterns   45

3.3   Number of Behavior Patterns and Names of
Dominant Behavior Patterns by Class   46

3.4   Distributions of Segment Features   54

3.5   High Frequency Segment Patterns   64

4.1   Distribution and Mean Involvement of
Cognitive Levels by Pacing   80

4.2   Mean Involvement by Complexity of
Cognitive Levels   84

4.3   Mean Involvement by Type of Pacing   85

4.4   Distribution of Formats in Teacher-Paced
Segments at Factual Cognitive Level   88

4.5   Mean Involvement in Recitations at Different
Cognitive Levels   92

List of Figures

3.1 Mathematics Topics by Class ($N = 20$)   32

3.2 Social Studies Topics by Class ($N = 19$)   36

3.3 Materials Used in Mathematics ($N = 20$) and
Social Studies ($N = 19$) Classes   50

3.4 Pacing Distributions in Mathematics and Social
Studies Segments   52

3.5 Ratio of Teacher/Child Pacing in Two
Subjects for Individual Teachers   71

Preface

Many educational researchers and nonprofessionals see the elementary school day as humdrum and uniform—broken primarily by recesses and lunch. That researchers most frequently study classroom settings in which teachers actively lead instruction has contributed to the perception of school experience as uniform in character. Certain kinds of data (for example, the ratio of teacher talk to student talk measured at different times in the school day) have also bolstered the assumption of sameness in daily school experience. The research described in this book, however, shows such ready and uncritical assumptions to be untenable. Variation in classroom practice is revealed with the systematic, detailed, and multifaceted view of instructional activity described here. More specifically, and more important, instructional arrangements change with the subject taught. The topic influences both the design and the enactment of classroom experiences. In this book, I document these subject matter differences and consider their possible origins and consequences.

Primary financial support for the research was provided by the National Institute of Education (contract no. 400-77-0094). Most of the data were collected during 1979, and some additional classes were observed in 1981. J. Alan Thomas and I received funding for a somewhat unusual collaboration that involved recruiting school districts and conducting fieldwork to serve both our research goals. We worked together through the data-collection period, but each of us had independent research projects to which the data related. A scholar concerned with the microeconomics of education and school finance and a classroom researcher do not often attain such close scholarly ties, but the arrangement proved profitable and satisfying in this case. It also broadened the type of data available to both of us.

Other financial support for data collection was provided by the Biomedical Research Support Grant Program at the University of

Chicago in 1981 (PHS 5 S07 RR-07029-14). The Spencer Foundation generously supported my fellowship at the Center for Advanced Study in the Behavioral Sciences at Stanford during the 1984–85 academic year, when I accomplished much of the writing of this book. Some of the conceptual work on the role of textbooks in instruction was supported by a research grant from the Spencer Foundation. I also received funds from the Benton Center for Curriculum and Instruction at the University of Chicago during the final preparation of the manuscript.

The research would not have been possible without the willingness of teachers, administrators, parents, and children to open their doors to us and spend time with us. Although their identities must remain confidential, I express my thanks to all the persons who let us study them.

A project of this scope and duration can only be accomplished with the help and cooperation of many people. A number of graduate students assumed major responsibility for the ongoing activities of the project, particularly during the fieldwork period. The care, intelligence, and commitment that Fran Kemmerer and Terry Ferguson displayed are impossible to measure. They both were involved with the project through the coding and analysis of data. I am grateful to them for their personal and intellectual contributions to the research.

We recruited an especially able group of field-workers who conducted observations in classrooms and interviews with parents. Some also helped code the data. Perhaps starting in a famous Chicago blizzard helped to build the camaraderie and professionalism that were characteristic of the group. The field-workers, many of them students in the Department of Education, were Rosalba Castaneda, Joy Dorsch, Janna Dresden, Chris Gruber, Ruth Jones, Jackie Kirley, Jane Plihal, Nancy Sonenfield, Pauline Urton, and Sherwood Wang. Jane Plihal also conducted teacher interviews. Through the observation period, Robyn Beatty, in her role as project secretary and coordinator, helped tremendously. Julie Less was project secretary through most of the writing of reports and other documents. Her competence, patience, and editorial skills are most appreciated.

Christa Winter served as a research assistant through the data-coding, analysis, and writing stages. She has been of great intellectual help and has also kept data, literature, and other materials in working order. I value her analytic skills and her care.

Sarah Tahsler-Patton also served as a research assistant after the project data had been collected and helped to acquaint me with the literature on peer groups. Sheila Graybeal provided valuable research assistance in the later stages of the project. Arthur Burke was the major statistical analyst for the project. Early on, Betsy Becker also helped with statistical work. At various times, Dave Rogosa and Larry Hedges offered valuable statistical consultation.

The preparation of this manuscript was aided by the stimulating, nurturant climate of the Center for Advanced Study in Behavioral Sciences. Anna Tower, who word-processed the text, brought competence, experience, and a smile to the task. Deanna Knickerbocker created the figures and tables with skill. Muriel Bell provided very helpful editorial suggestions on a number of chapters.

The final version of the manuscript was completed at the University of Chicago. During the last burst of revisionary energy, I was extremely fortunate to have the assistance of Diane Bowers in the Benton Center for Curriculum and Instruction in the Department of Education. Diane helped produce the final copy of the manuscript with good cheer as well as excellent word-processing skills.

A number of colleagues deserve thanks. The help and insight of Alan Thomas, were critical at the inception of research and important at other times as well. I would not have undertaken a project that involved such extensive recruiting of school districts had he not spearheaded the effort. I fondly recall our many visits to schools to enlist cooperation or to get a firsthand view of facilities. As work progressed, his keen interest and perspective proved extremely valuable.

Jacqueline Goodnow used some of her precious fellowship time at the Center at Stanford to carefully read the manuscript and suggest ways it could be strengthened. I also appreciate the careful reading given the manuscript by Larry Cuban of Stanford University. He provided both helpful suggestions and stimulating conversation on topics covered in the book. My colleagues at Chicago, Meg Gallagher, Susan Goldin-Meadow, Philip Jackson, and Jim Stigler, also offered useful comments on the manuscript and its content.

My 1983 final report to the National Institute of Education, *Classroom activity structures in the fifth grade*, might be considered the first draft of this book, as it contains many of the results reported here. Some of the results have also appeared in journal articles and book chapters. In particular, I acknowledge use of material reported in my 1983 chapter, "An ecological perspective on classroom instruction: Implications for teacher education," which appeared in P. Tamir, A. Hofstein, and M. Ben-Peretz, eds., *Preservice and inservice training of science teachers* (Philadelphia: Balaban International Sciences Services). I also reported results in my 1984 article, "Teacher evaluation: The limits of looking" (*Educational Researcher,* 13 (9): 11–18).

Last, I thank my children, Amalia and Daniel, who responded to my findings with the perspective of students in schools ("For this they pay you money, Mom?"), but to my efforts with affection and enthusiasm. They are discerning critics but ever staunch supporters.

1

Subject Matter, Classroom Activity, and Student Involvement

INTRODUCTION

With respect to classroom activity, the subject matters. Instruction is not the same all day long. This book demonstrates that what is being taught profoundly shapes instructional activity.

We have come a long way in recognizing the role of context in human affairs. But we seem to forget it when thinking about education. In our search for ideal methods of teaching and effective schools, we accept the mistaken assumption that sameness pervades classroom activity. We seek a pattern of actions that characterize the effective teacher, and ascribe consistent styles to teachers.

But on the contrary, individual teachers arrange instruction very differently depending on what they are teaching. Their pedagogical practices are not stable. The belief that teachers are consistently good or bad may be valid for a few, but it is unquestionably wrong for many.

A detailed examination of elementary math and social studies lessons and students' reactions to them provides the empirical basis for our claims. Our method involved direct observations of the classroom activity structure, which enabled us to account for the actions of all participants in a particular time and place. Our method captured instructional arrangements, not just teaching. We examined not only teacher-student interactions but also the classroom setting as it was arranged and used by students and teachers during lessons.

Such systematic scrutiny of activities revealed the many ways in which classroom experience differs when various subjects are taught, even though the same teacher is in charge. We paid particular attention to instructional formats, the nature of the intellectual goals sought in lessons, and the activities that went on when children worked under direct teacher supervision, on their own, or with one another.

In this work we ask: How is instruction carried out in mathematics and social studies classes? In what ways is instruction in the two fields the same, and in what ways different? What classroom activities take place? What instructional formats are used—for example, recitation, seatwork, small-group work, or contests? When instruction is divided into activity segments, what intellectual goals are addressed in the segments? What are students expected to learn? How do students accomplish their tasks? Do they work on their own, do they cooperate, or do they work with the teacher? What materials do they use? What, if any, choices do they make?

Particular attention is paid to the conditions under which different intellectual goals are pursued. For example, what kinds of cognitive learning are involved when the teacher is actively directing an instructional segment? Are the same intellectual goals pursued when students work on their own as when they cooperate? Are the same educational conditions found when students are expected to learn facts, apply concepts, or become proficient in research skills?

Describing classroom action and its connection to subject matter was our first purpose. Equally important was our second goal: to understand how students react to instruction. Involvement in classroom activities served as our gauge of student response. We found that the same students were not consistently involved or uninvolved in the presence of a given teacher. Rather, what went on in lessons and how activities were structured affected student involvement.

We ask: How are levels of pupils' involvement related to the conditions under which they work? Does the type of learning required affect student involvement? In particular, how is student involvement correlated with the complexity of educational goals? Does challenge enhance or diminish students' engagement? Does student response differ in the presence of messages containing needed, as opposed to redundant, information? Are students more attentive when under continuous teacher supervision, when left to work on their own, or when they collaborate?

A picture of the responsive student was drawn with the help of our data. We found that students were efficient—they attended to information when it was needed in the flow of instruction, and they listened to novel information. They were engaged by complexity, as they exhibited higher levels of involvement when asked to perform more intellectually complex activities than when given less challenging, simpler chores. Students also responded positively to other students—they were particularly engaged when cooperating with one another.

Our view of the conditions that elicit high levels of student engagement does not always square with current recommendations for effective teaching. The students we studied did not always behave in ways that some investigators would have expected. We explain these new findings primarily by considering how we studied the classrooms, whom we studied, and what we studied. Of special importance was our examination of the same pupils studying different subjects with the same teacher, and our examination of classroom activity as a whole.

The *ways* in which children learn subjects, in fact, may be a more important object of study than what they learn. Specific facts and content mastered in school are rather quickly forgotten. On the other hand, ideas about how you learn something—indeed whether you think you can learn it—are more likely to endure. Those ideas are formulated, nurtured, and sustained in school through patterns of activity that are experienced over and over again. We have studied those activities and pupils' responses to them.

SUBJECT MATTER AND INSTRUCTION

How might subject matter influence the form of instruction? To begin with, the kinds of things we want children to learn in a given subject can constrain the ways in which it could be taught and learned. For instance, in matters of physical skill, direct practice rather than vicarious experience is needed. Creative work, however, may be better encouraged through discussion and brainstorming.

Connections between the goals of instruction and the means have not been studied comprehensively across school subjects. However, the issue is addressed in many specific research studies that compare different educational methods. Comparisons of alternative methods of reading (Chall 1977) or heuristic and other approaches to teaching mathematical problem solving (Silver 1985) are examples of research that could be used to develop a better general understanding of the fit between specific educational means and particular kinds of successful learning. Studies of the specific effects of informal or open education in contrast to teacher-centered classrooms (Horwitz 1979) might also be germane. Although we cannot synthesize the many studies that compare teaching methods, we will address the problem of fit between educational ends and means by examining instruction in two school subjects with different educational objectives.

It is likely that certain types of knowledge and goals are associated with (or even require) particular instructional approaches. The skills, abilities, and attitudes students are expected to develop in math and social studies are quite distinct. If different goals involve different instructional means, teachers ought to arrange classrooms as a function of the goals. The result should be different kinds of instruction in lessons devoted to each of our study subjects.

The perceived importance or priority of a subject may influence both the quantity and quality of instruction accorded it. In American schools, certain fields are considered basic for elementary school pupils, and others less essential. Distinctions between "basic" and "enrichment" subjects—or "skills" and "frills"—have been made for a long time. Perhaps with some justification, proponents of an integrated approach to instruction oppose the distinctions since they promote an undesirable compartmentalization of knowledge. There is, however, a logic to the argument that some subjects are basic in the sense of being indispensable to the acquisition of more advanced learning. For example, reading is considered essential because it is prerequisite to learning in other fields. Mathematics holds a similar place.

A look at the accountability system will frequently reveal whether a subject has high priority. External testing programs (usually norm-referenced standardized tests) are regularly administered in language arts and mathematics but not in such enrichment fields as social studies or science. More teacher-made tests are also administered in basic subjects. The existence of accountability pressure reinforces the "basic" status of these fields but also results from it. Thus, testing programs and perceptions of the importance of fields of study are mutually reinforcing, and together they influence the goals and shape of classroom instruction. A very significant effect of testing programs is a narrowing of educational objectives to conform to those in tests. More uniform instructional goals are likely to be found in the heavily tested basic school subjects such as mathematics.

There are documentable differences in the amount of instruction in basic and enrichment fields. Together, priority and grade level determine time allocations to subjects. Reading and language arts activities receive the most attention in the primary grades. Math ranks second (Weiss 1978). Other subjects, such as social studies and science, are taught very infrequently or not at all in the first years of school.

In the upper elementary grades, time allocations shift. Reading instruction still commands the most time, but mathematics time increases. Weiss (1978) reports that approximately one and a half hours are spent daily in reading instruction in K–3, and about one hour in grades 4–6. Some teachers allocate time to science and social studies in the upper grades, while others allocate none. It is not unusual for a child to complete the first six grades of school with little if any instruction in science, social studies, and other enrichment areas.

Time allocation is but one indicator of the priority assigned a subject. More relevant to this inquiry is the degree to which instructional methods believed to maximize achievement are used. Such approaches give attention to individual differences in student ability and aptitudes, and focus more consistently on the progress of individual pupils. Instruction that is more differentiated and responsive to the learning needs of individual pupils is found more often in basic subjects.

Perhaps the best examples of such practices are teacher-led reading groups in the primary grades. While a teacher works with a small group, she can provide effective individual attention to novice readers, but the rest of the class is provided only minimal supervision. Teacher-led small groups cannot occupy too much of the school day because they would produce a net loss of learning. Since small groups are deemed essential in reading in the primary grades, their use in other fields is sharply curtailed. In math, within-class ability grouping is seen infrequently in the primary grades, but is used more often in the upper elementary grades when it becomes more feasible. Across the grades, instructional procedures that bring students to required achievement levels are more apparent in reading and math than in fields like social studies and science.

Another way in which subject matter may influence instruction is in the extent to which the field is structured and sequential. Math, in contrast to many other school subjects, is highly structured and sequential. Certain forms of instruction may be more compatible with sequential fields than with less-ordered disciplines. For instance, fields with a clear sequence seem especially suited for individualized programs in which children work through a set of materials on their own and for computer-assisted instruction or mastery learning.

When there is a lack of sequence in a field of study, curriculum development may be difficult. Ellis (1981), discussing elementary social studies, notes

> Perhaps no other area of the elementary school curriculum poses a greater problem to those who develop curriculum than social studies. . . . In what order should students study certain groups of people? Should groups of people be studied chronologically? Regionally? In mathematics, most would agree that addition precedes division as a learning experience. But does Mexico precede Canada? (pp. 24–25).

Ellis focuses on the problem of content selection in nonsequential fields. Diversity of content may also lead to diversity in materials and in instructional modes.

Related to the properties of structure and sequence—but by no means identical to them—is the extent to which a school subject is clearly defined and delineated. Some fields of study are fairly well defined and circumscribed, while the scope of others is less sharp, and the lack of definition may have instructional ramifications. The subjects we studied, math and social studies, contrast in just this way. Social studies is not a well-defined school subject, but math is.

Subject matter differences in instruction may also result directly from differing recommendations for pedagogy in the subject fields. As early as the beginning of the century, psychologists developed recommendations for instruction based on their analysis of different psychological processes in different fields of study (Freeman 1916). Now the persons who train elementary school teachers in teaching mathematics, science, social studies, and so forth are usually subject matter specialists themselves. If there are traditions or beliefs about suitable teaching practices in particular fields, these are likely to be transmitted to neophytes even if the trainers do so subconsciously. In fact, different assumptions do seem present in the pedagogy espoused for different school subjects, a point brought out by looking at textbooks used in teacher-training courses and teachers' guides provided with student textbooks (Graybeal and Stodolsky 1986).

Thus, subject matter seems to shape instructional practice for several reasons. The nature of the knowledge itself, the structure and sequence of the discipline, and the desired goals all affect pedagogy. Other influences include the value placed on the subject, whether it is considered basic or enrichment, whether performance is assessed externally, and the degree of definition the school subject has. In addition, though elementary school teachers are generalists, the pedagogical training they receive in various disciplines apparently embodies different principles and ways of teaching.

For all these reasons, a careful examination of how teachers teach different school subjects seems important and is overdue. We selected fifth-grade mathematics and social studies for study because they contrast in most of the ways we have discussed. Math is considered basic, social studies for enrichment. As taught, they differ in goals and objectives, degree of sequence and structure, underlying discipline, degree of definition, and prevalence of external testing.

Mathematics Programs

Arithmetic is the heart of the mathematics curriculum in American elementary schools, and skill in computation is the primary goal. During the period of our observations, the textbooks in wide use across the country had similar sequences of topics. Math in the primary grades consisted almost exclusively of numbers, numeration, place value, addition, subtraction, and multiplication with whole numbers. In the intermediate grades, the work concerned multiplication, division, decimals, and fractions. Most books contained units on measurement and geometry.

In every elementary grade level, students typically spend the first months of the school year reviewing operations studied in prior years (Flanders 1987). In comparison to content coverage in the textbooks of other countries, American texts introduce mathematical content very gradually. By the end of elementary school, our students have been exposed to much less mathematical content than their age mates in Eastern Europe or Japan (Raizen and Jones 1985). American students particularly lack experience in a variety of problem-solving skills (e.g., different types of word problems), estimation, mental calculation, solid geometry, real-world applications, and measurement. While many math educators are proponents of problem solving and analysis, most instruction is geared to algorithmic learning (Bell and Bell 1983; Fey 1979; Stake and Easley 1978; Romberg and Carpenter 1986).

Curricula were radically revised in the "new math" era of the 1960s to include mathematics, not simply arithmetic. Understanding mathematical thinking and the logic and concepts underlying calculation was another major departure. The use of manipulatives and reliance on concrete objects for introducing concepts to students were also stressed. By the time of our study, however, new math had been declared a failure. The books returned to more, but not an exclusive, emphasis on arithmetic. However, a residual legacy of the new math may be detected in content changes in textbooks— for example, frequent inclusion of geometry, probability, measurement, or logic. Interestingly, in the 1980s we are critically reexamining the mathematics curriculum, with renewed attention to some of the concerns raised in earlier curriculum revisions.

What do fifth graders study in math? After review, they learn primarily mathematical operations with fractional numbers and decimals. During the course of the year, most students are exposed to addition and subtraction of fractional numbers, including renaming mixed numerals; whole number times a fractional number, fractional number times a fractional number, mixed numeral times whole number, and division as multiplication with reciprocal. Operations with decimals include multiplication and division of tenths, hundredths, and thousandths by whole numbers. Depending on the text they use, fifth graders may also study area and volume and learn how to determine the perimeter of certain polygons. They may study triangles and be introduced to right, scalene, isosceles, equilateral, congruent, and similar triangles. They may also study scale drawing and the concept of probability. Some problem-solving exercises, usually involving operations with fractions, are also found in textbooks.

Social Studies Programs

It is not easy to specify exactly what constitutes the "standard" social studies curriculum for the elementary grades. A list of disciplines including history, geography, government (civics), sociology, economics, and anthropology are represented in various social studies programs, although history, geography, and government are most common. From a topical and disciplinary point of view there are debates about what the primary focus of social studies instruction should be. Specialists debate what disciplines should be represented, whether and how programs can be more relevant to society, and whether students should have experiences with actual social science methods, such as collecting and analyzing data. The competing demands of citizenship education, a curriculum developed around social needs, and programs that serve disciplinary goals have not yet been adjudicated.

Although a set of uniform topics cannot be said to reflect what is taught in elementary social studies, many programs are organized on the "expanding environment" principle. Children begin in kindergarten or first grade with studies of their immediate social environment (the family) and then progress through studies of their neighborhoods, communities, state, country, and the world by the end of elementary school. As Jarolimek (1977) notes, most programs also cover current events, holidays, and some special units such as career education, law-related education, or family education.

At the fifth-grade level, the focus is usually on the United States. The year typically includes study of Native Americans, the history of the settlement and expansion of the country, and United States geography and natural resources. Students may also learn about our neighbors: Canada, Mexico, and Latin America. In the state of Illinois, career education is a mandated topic for fifth graders regardless of what social studies program their school has adopted.

The objectives of social studies programs are very diverse, but there are some points of consensus. Most programs address the American heritage and democracy, attempting to prepare students for their responsibilities as citizens. A certain amount of factual knowledge, usually about history, government, and geography, is also expected. As a secondary agenda, social studies programs may hone reading skills, especially in the early grades. Later on, social studies programs stress students' abilities to find information in a variety of sources. Some programs emphasize inquiry and critical thinking; others pursue social and affective goals along with cognitive outcomes. Thus, inquiry, research skills, interpersonal problem solving, values clarification, and knowledge are all desired outcomes of some social studies programs (Ellis 1981; Orlandi 1971).

During the 1960s a variety of curricula was developed under the umbrella of the "new social studies." The new programs were diverse but tended to incorporate disciplines beyond history and geography, include regions from the non-Western world, and espouse goals such as the development of inquiry and values clarification. They frequently recommended such instructional approaches as small-group work, active learning, and simulations rather than primary reliance on textbooks (Jarolimek 1981; Morrissett 1982).

Jarolimek (1981) asserts that social studies instruction was in disarray in the 1970s and the "new social studies" did not have a long-term impact. However, others argue that some changes in textbook content have been lasting, although instructional approach has remained fairly static (Morrissett 1982; Weiss 1978).

At this time, multidisciplinary programs organized around comprehensive themes or problems are most prevalent in elementary schools (Superka, Hawke, and Morrissett 1980). For instance, in a series developed by the Center for the Study of Instruction (CSI) in San Francisco, which we saw in use in one of our classes, such themes as "human behavior is shaped by the social environment," and "economic behavior depends upon the utilization of resources" are addressed in different form at every grade level. A strong disciplinary flavor, characteristic of the "new" social studies, is evident in the CSI series.

The *Man and His World* series, published by Noble and Noble, is also thematic. As stated in the teacher's edition for the fifth grade, three themes are emphasized:

the diversity of groups within the country, the relation of people to the land and the growth of the American economy, and the examination of the past (1974, p. TE14).

The series incorporates original sources so that students can evaluate evidence and develop inquiry skills, but it also stresses reading skills and knowledge objectives. The fifth-grade text, *Many Americans—One Nation,* was used in one of our classes.

Another thematic, "new" social studies program that we saw in use is *Man: A Course of Study (MACOS).* It focuses on what it means to be human, comparing the life cycle and social organization of man and other species. A Darwinian account of the evolution of man is part of the program—a controversial feature in some school districts. The program, developed by Education Development Center, incorporates anthropological techniques and data in student learning experiences and includes intensive studies of salmon, baboons, and Eskimos. The program uses films and replicas of artifacts as well as activities planned for small work groups.

The field of social studies has been bounded and conceived in many different ways by educators; there is room for many enactments of instruction under this name. We shall demonstrate that, although there is a certain amount of concordance in social studies programs around the country, there is much variety in what is taught and how instruction is organized.

THE ACTIVITY STRUCTURE AND ACTIVITY SEGMENTS

Since we wanted to describe classroom activity as a whole, in units easily recognized by teachers and students, we chose the activity structure and its component activity segments as our basic units of study. The activity structure is in fact how classroom tasks are organized in a lesson. The organization is revealed by the activity segments that occur at any one time.

The choice of a sampling unit can be an acute problem in classroom research. If one is interested in studying instruction through a period such as a lesson, it is important to capture the major divisions of instructional activity as they unfold. The segment, a concept akin to that of a behavior setting, was originally defined and studied by ecological psychologists (Barker 1968; Gump 1967; Ross 1984). Activity segments are the major divisions of lessons.

In essence, an activity segment is a part of a lesson that has a focus or concern and starts and stops. A segment has a particular instructional format, participants, materials, and behavioral expectations and goals. It occupies a certain block of time in a lesson and occurs in a fixed physical setting. A segment's focus can be instructional or managerial. We have studied only instructional segments in detail. However, transitions (managerial segments) have been studied by others (Arlin 1979).

A description of an activity structure and its component activity segments catalogues the salient aspects of the physical environment and the persons present (teachers, aides, pupils). A description of a lesson in progress also portrays the main tasks or activities in which the children and teacher are engaged. We need to know how each activity is structured, who is present, the activity's duration, its instructional purpose and format, and the materials in use.

For example, an observation of a primary class reading lesson might show two main activities for a twenty-minute period: (1) a group of eight children seated at the front of the room in a circle of chairs, supervised by the teacher, taking turns reading certain pages in the basal reader; (2) a group of eighteen children working at their desks in a phonics workbook, writing answers to written questions about the "th" blend. Although this sketch omits many details that our empirical descriptions of activity include, we can identify two segments: a reading circle in a recitation format and a simultaneously operating seatwork segment. Thus, the activity structure contains all activity segments occurring at a given time.

Segments can occur singly or, as in the example just given, simultaneously with one or more other segments. Segments are of various lengths, and the duration of an activity segment is an important property. Using activity segments permits analysis of instructional arrangements of varying durations, perhaps in a more useful way than with commonly used systems that observe for fixed time intervals. For instance, from an instructional point of view, two recitation segments of different lengths may be very similar and can be analyzed together in a study of segments.

Burns (1984), in a review of studies about classroom activity, identifies key elements associated with the research on activity segments. He suggests that a complete description of an academic activity requires information on the learning task to be accomplished and the activity format—how the work is organized and who does what. Our observations provided that kind of information. (The observation procedures are fully described in chapter 2.)

A primary conceptual appeal of activity segments is their salience and their congruity with the way teachers think about conducting lessons. Studies of teacher planning (Clark and Yinger 1979) indicate that teachers think about instruction in terms of content, activities, and pedagogical routines—features very similar to those studied in an analysis of activity segments. The unit of analysis used in this research will enable us to avoid parsing instructional activity into small bits, a practice followed frequently in the past. Instead we examine regularities and variation in instruction in meaningful and easily identified parts of lessons.

Segment Properties

Features of activity segments are described and analysed in this research in order to develop a detailed picture of instructional activity and to answer some central questions. The segment features we examined include some studied previously (Gump 1967; Grannis and Jackson 1973; Grannis 1978) and others developed or adapted for this study.

We began by characterizing each segment by its instructional format—a global and familiar set of categories for well-known instructional arrangements. Recitation, seatwork, group work, demonstration, and student reports are all examples of formats. We also identified the main student behavior pattern expected in each segment. Solving problems at one's desk, answering questions, reading orally, listening, and watching a film were among the student behaviors categorized. Easily recognized coding categories were set up for both instructional formats and student behavior patterns.

Two segment properties, pacing and cognitive level, are paramount in our analysis, particularly as it relates to student reactions to instruction. Pacing was identified by both Gump (1967) and Grannis (1978) as a pivotal setting variable and enters into most discussions of educational arrangements.

Pacing indicates who sets the rate of work during a segment. In our codes, we distinguished four pacing conditions: teacher, child, cooperative (child-child), and mechanical (audiovisual). Different pacing conditions probably require variation in other segment features for optimal educational effect. Along these lines, Grannis (1978) proposed that options, feedback, and student interaction are among the segment features that must be congruent with pacing to produce high levels of student involvement and learning. For instance, a congruent child-paced setting would be one in which the students chose their activities (options), had materials such as manipulatives that provided feedback or correction, and were allowed to work with other pupils or obtain help from other students (student interaction). According to Grannis, seatwork, a common child-paced setting, is often incongruent because students do not choose activities or have access to feedback, and interaction between children is frequently forbidden. In fact, prior studies (Gump 1967; Grannis 1978; Stallings 1975), mostly at the primary level, have usually found that students have difficulty maintaining high involvement levels in seatwork.

The extent to which students should take responsibility for their own learning is a pivotal choice around which debates about educational practice have been waged. Who should pace learning, how tasks and topics to be studied should be chosen, and the nature of the intellectual goals of schooling are dimensions addressed with different educational strategies depending on the analysts' starting points. For example, educators who are inclined to view the child as intrinsically motivated to learn often suggest that more autonomy be given students in a well-prepared learning environment (e.g.,

Hawkins 1974). Similarly, scholars who value collective action in learning (e.g., Dewey 1899; Slavin 1983) applaud schools in which children and adults learn together or children collaborate. On the other hand, researchers working in the process-product tradition have tended to recommend teacher-centered practices such as the direct instruction model (Rosenshine 1979).

We will join this issue by examining classroom activity under different pacing conditions. We will ask how segments are divided into those paced by the teacher, by children working alone, by children working together, or by films or other audiovisual aids or electronic devices. Of special importance is our analysis of how intellectual goals and pacing are coordinated. What tasks are students asked to accomplish under teacher direction, on their own, and collaboratively? Finally, we will investigate student response and involvement under different pacing conditions.

In order to investigate cognitive level, we coded the inferred intellectual goal of each segment. We developed a hierarchy of cognitive levels based on a modification of categories from the *Taxonomy of Educational Objectives* (Bloom et al. 1956) and categories identified by Orlandi (1971), who described objectives of social studies programs. The hierarchy is based on complexity, the dimension underlying the original *Taxonomy*. The least complex objectives, aside from those with no cognitive goal, are those involving factual recall or learning. Next in the hierarchy fall those that involve learning concepts and skills and comprehension of reading materials. Generally, above those goals are the categories that deal with the development of research skills, including the use of symbolic and graphic materials. Finally, application and other higher mental processes are deemed most complex.

With the use of these codes, we could ascertain the different intellectual goals that students addressed in math and social studies. In this connection, we could compare the intellectual quality of work in the schools we observed with the quality observed in other studies. We could also determine the conditions under which students worked toward different cognitive goals, particularly by looking at the relationship of pacing and cognitive level. Further, we were especially interested in student involvement as it relates to the complexity of learning tasks—a factor believed very important.

In addition to instructional format, student behavior pattern, pacing, and cognitive level, we examined a number of other segment features already mentioned in passing. In particular, we coded the nature of student options, expected levels of student interaction, feedback available to students, and the role the teacher played in each segment. We also ascertained the location of students during segments and coded the materials used by both students and teacher. Specific coding categories for these variables, which assist in rounding out the descriptive portrait of activity segments, are presented along with our findings in chapter 3, and defined with examples in appendix B.

Much of the research that has investigated student involvement, achievement, and classroom activity has been restricted to skill subjects, frequently in the early grades. We have the opportunity to expand our knowledge about students' responses to instruction by going beyond studies of young children in reading and math to fifth-grade math and social studies. The inclusion of a basic and an enrichment field will allow further assessment of how instruction looks in schools. It will also provide additional data with which to assess some strong claims about the efficacy of certain instructional arrangements, such as the direct instruction model (Rosenshine 1979).

STUDENT INVOLVEMENT

Every segment in which sample children participated has an associated estimate of student involvement, expressed as the percentage of observations coded as "on-task" out of all observations of students made during the segment. Students were considered "on-task" if their observable behavior was in line with expectations in that setting. Average involvement rates can be used to compare the degree to which settings of particular kinds involve students in the planned activities.

Learning is related to the way in which students spend time in classrooms (Stodolsky 1972; Anderson 1984). Overt conformity with setting expectations is not a direct measure of student attainment or thought processes. Children are not certain to learn if they listen to a teacher's lecture, do a seatwork assignment, or cooperate on a common project with others, but learning is more likely if they are attentive. Student involvement does not secure learning, but it is usually a necessary step. Though high levels of involvement may be found in settings that are not productive for students' learning or growth, we assume that higher involvement rates usually occur in more effective educational environments. We use student involvement, measured by direct observation, as an index of response to the educational setting while recognizing that attention must be deployed to the right purposes.

An overt measure of student involvement is probably a better indicator of underlying intellectual processes and learning in some situations than in others. When observable task actions are direct signs of student practice and success—as is the case when the required action pattern is itself overt—involved behavior is more likely to indicate learning. In activities that involve passive reception, as when children listen to a teacher lecture, overt signs of attention are probably less closely tied to student learning. The closer a measure of involvement is to an actual component of learning the more likely it is to be a good index of learning. [1]

It is possible to examine the way in which students respond to various segment features by using our estimates of student involvement. Some setting characteristics may be more "attractive" or interesting to students than others. We proposed that the level of students' on-task behavior would change in response to features of information in segments and to the curricular function of a segment in the flow of a lesson. More specifically, we proposed that the complexity of information, the novelty of information, and the need for information would all relate to student involvement. Beyond the type of information in segments, their social arrangements were also believed to condition student response. In particular, we believed upper-elementary students would find working with one another more engaging than working alone or under teacher supervision.

We will examine certain segment varieties, particularly categories of pacing and cognitive level, for systematic trends in student involvement. We will also identify sets of segments, such as those meant to prepare pupils for subsequent tasks, that can shed light on students' responses to the quality of information contained in them.

Background on Student Involvement

Kounin (1970), in his ground-breaking book on classroom management and discipline, showed that students respond collectively to such aspects of the teacher's lesson flow as momentum and smoothness. Kounin and Gump (1974) showed that the signal systems of lessons that possessed continuity, insulation, and lack of intrusiveness produced higher involvement in preschool children. Analogously, we believe students respond to the quality of information a segment contains. Their response is conditioned by at least two important features: the complexity of the information, and the necessity or novelty of the information. [2]

With regard to complexity, it is proposed that students become more involved in cognitively complex tasks than in those lower in the cognitive level hierarchy. We argue that more complex tasks evoke more student attention for a number of reasons. We believe cognitively complex tasks are generally more challenging for students; they are usually more difficult than simple work such as obtaining facts. Thus, more actual mental effort and attention would seem required to achieve complex goals. We also believe that complex tasks are intrinsically more interesting to pupils than low-level intellectual activities. Acting on this interest, students should be more willing and more motivated to attend to cognitively complex tasks than to those at a lower level.

Thus, our expectation that student involvement will be graded to match the complexity of their assigned tasks arises from considering the actual effort a given task requires, as well as the interest or motivational value of different activities. We expected higher levels of involvement when students pursued application and higher mental processes than when they were asked to process factual information. We disagree with the supporters of the direct instruction model in their belief that low-level questioning and low-level tasks are the most appropriate or involving for children. Instead, we side with those who assert that challenging and complex activity promotes growth in students.

The need for information in the flow of a lesson can be assessed by considering whether what is being communicated is likely to be known already or easily garnered in other ways, or on the other hand carries information required for task completion and not likely to be available in other ways. Preparatory segments in which directions are given to students can be examined in this light, as can checking work and review segments. When such segments contain information that students already know—for example, the assignment is written on the board even though the teacher gives it orally—we would expect lower attention levels than when the teacher is the only source of information about an upcoming task.

If students are less likely to pay close attention when information is predictable or redundant, they will probably be more attentive and interested when information is novel. In a very general way, we could pick out activities or messages that were unusual in a given setting, and we expected that students would take particular note of them. We did not thoroughly test this assumption but did keep novelty in mind when analyzing student involvement patterns.

In general, we predicted that students would expend energy and attention according to principles of behavioral efficiency. We assumed that students would adjust their collective response to a setting as the information or tasks required. Students know when their full attention is needed, and average involvement rates will reflect this knowledge. The naive assumption that student involvement or attention should always be high neglects the more fundamental proposition that good human functioning involves spending energy as needed. If less than full attention is adequate for the task, why expend more?

The appropriateness of the internal arrangements of an educational setting for the age and learning histories of pupils may also affect student involvement. As noted earlier, child-paced settings, particularly seatwork, have been shown to produce low levels of involvement among primary children; when young students work under direct teacher supervision, they pay more attention. These primary grade findings are bolstered by the data used to formulate the direct instruction model (Rosenshine 1979). There, teacher-directed lessons emerged as the most effective in studies of current practice in skill classes for young children.

A plausible hypothesis, tested with support by Grannis (1978), is that the overall conditions under which the seatwork is demanded are problematic, not simply that students are asked to work on their own. Low involvement is found in required, basic subjects in which little choice, interaction, and feedback are available. On the other hand, more internally consistent (or supportive) child-paced settings, found by Grannis much more frequently in enrichment subjects than in basic fields, are associated with higher student involvement.

In digesting these data on student responses to pacing arrangements in the primary grades, one detects a strong sense that children must be "made" to work. But the findings reviewed are mostly from traditional schools. The possibility of high involvement in child-paced settings in basic subjects should not be ruled out. More internally consistent seatwork activities, such as those found in enrichment subjects, might produce higher student involvement levels. How much the response to child pacing is a function of the students' age must be examined. Young children may be more involved in the teacher-paced condition because they are not yet capable of working on their own in a sustained manner. Older children may need less external support in the learning environment and less "prodding" to accomplish tasks. By examining differently paced segments, we were able to determine whether our fifth graders found child-paced settings similarly uninvolving.

Cooperative segments with extensive interaction between children have been almost nonexistent in the classes studied by previous researchers—particularly those studying the primary grades. The relatively narrow range of educational environments that have been investigated limits our understanding of the dynamics of student response to instruction, and was one motive for our investigation of math and social studies. However, prior data accurately reflect a paucity of group work and cooperative tasks in most elementary schools (Goodlad 1984; Stodolsky 1984a).

It is important to know how students respond to cooperative arrangements when they are part of their regular school experience. Given children's strong interests (if not preoccupation) in their peers, we would expect collaborative work to positively engage them. When cooperative segments occurred in our classes, we examined them to address this issue for its special interest.

One last consideration regarding student involvement in instruction should be mentioned. Some previous research, such as Grannis's, has found students more involved in enrichment than in basic subjects. This distinction reminds us that interest in the content of an activity relates to student involvement, and that we must assess the different student response to our two subjects. Of course, interest may be conditioned by the subject matter itself, by the goals of instruction, by the arrangements used to teach the subject, and perhaps by the pressures associated with accomplishment in the field. But we think that the conditions of learning are more directly related to student involvement than to the field of study as such.

In the next chapter we will describe our methods. Findings on subject matter and curricular differences in activity segments will be presented in chapter 3. The coordination of intellectual activity and pacing, along with analyses of student involvement, are presented in chapter 4. Our last chapter is reserved for discussion, conclusions, and implications. In it, we will pay special attention to the routes to learning provided students through different classroom activities and how students develop ideas about the meaning of learning. These important consequences of schooling are considered in light of our demonstration that specific activities are tied to the subject taught.

2

Research Methods

The sample of classrooms in which we observed math and social studies came from eleven school districts in the Chicago standard metropolitan sampling area, including the city of Chicago. The districts were a random stratified sample selected by the amount of money spent per pupil on schooling and by community socioeconomic status.[1] Districts were located in low-, middle-, and high-status communities. Table 2.1 contains descriptive information on the sample.

The sample is not fully representative of all classrooms. For instance, classrooms in large urban systems and in small school districts were not studied in proportion to their numbers. However, the sample is demographically diverse enough to ensure instructional variety and includes a range of conditions in which fifth graders in a midwestern urban area attend school.[2]

SELECTION OF SCHOOLS, CLASSROOMS AND STUDENTS

Once a district agreed to participate, district superintendents identified schools that had socioeconomic characteristics typical of the district and principals willing to have their schools in the study. Within a participating district, we needed two fifth-grade classes in which to observe math and social studies instruction. The two classroom groups were usually in the same school, but occasionally in each of two district schools. The teachers were almost all volunteers, although a few seem to have been pressured by principals to participate. We tried to eliminate any highly unusual settings such as special education classes; otherwise classes entered the sample without regard to their student composition.

In our sample, classroom (or class) and teacher are not synonymous because self-contained classes, in which one teacher

Table 2.1. Sample Characteristics

Per Pupil Expenditure	Socioeconomic Status[a]		
	Low	Middle	High
Low ($1,271 and lower)	Cell 1 Districts = 2 Schools = 2 Classes = 6	Cell 2 Districts = 2 Schools = 2 Classes = 8	Cell 3 Districts = 0 Schools = 0 Classes = 0
High ($1,441 and higher)	Cell 4 Districts = 2 Schools = 2 Classes = 6	Cell 5 Districts = 2 Schools = 3 Classes = 7	Cell 6 Districts = 3 Schools = 4 Classes = 12

[a]Calculated with NORC occupational prestige ratings using parents' occupations in study classrooms. High is a score of 54 or greater, middle is 40–54, and scores below 40 are low. More detail on sample selection is in footnote 1, chapter 2.

oversees instruction in all subjects for a group of children, are not found uniformly at the fifth-grade level. Some schools have subject matter specialists teaching fifth graders, others have self-contained classes, and there are other variants. Our goal was to see the math and social studies instruction received by the same pupils, regardless of who was teaching them. Since a given group of students might be taught both subjects by the same teacher or by two different teachers, we use the convention of identifying classrooms by their subject matter content rather than by their teacher. Thus a group of children in the study was observed in two classes: their math class and their social studies class. In all, we observed twenty math classes and nineteen social studies classes taught by a total of twenty-one teachers. Fifteen teachers taught both math and social studies. The teachers who taught both subjects are identified with the letters A through O when referred to in the text or in tables and figures. Teachers who taught only one subject are identified with the letters P through U.

In each class, we observed eight students so as to estimate student involvement in the activities. Since our study was part of a larger data-collection effort, all parents of children in the classrooms were asked permission for their child to be observed and the child's records to be examined. Also, parents were themselves asked for interviews.[3] Students selected at random from each class list were placed in the sample if the necessary parental consents had been obtained. In most classes the sample observed was reasonably random. However, in a few cases the response rate was so poor that all or virtually all of the children with permission had to be used. Communities with lower socioeconomic status had lower rates of parental consent, perhaps because of the demands of the parent interview. However, standardized test scores available to us did not suggest that participants differed in ability from nonparticipants. In some classes the sample seemed to favor higher ability students, but more low ability youngsters were studied in other classes. There was no association between district characteristics and the tendency for higher or lower ability students to participate. Since students were observed in order to estimate the involvement levels of groups of pupils, we assume volunteer biases cancelled out.

DATA-COLLECTION PROCEDURES

In each class a pair of researchers worked together to make direct observations; they obtained descriptions of math and social studies activities and estimates of student involvement. There were eleven field-workers, most of them graduate students or experienced teachers. During a three-week period preceding the data collection, they were trained to establish mastery of the activity structure recording system and the method for observing individual students' behavior. Other background and descriptive information about the classes and teachers was also gathered by field staff.[4] All teachers were interviewed.[5] Data collection took place in the second half of the school year, from late January through May.

Observations of Classroom Activity and Students

Observers were usually in a class for three weeks. During the first few days, maps were drawn, children's names were learned, and observers became familiar with classroom resources and routines. The first week served as a period of acclimatization for researchers, teachers, and students.[6]

The classroom activities described in this report were observed in two consecutive weeks in each classroom. Observers were available to record ten consecutive days of full math and social studies lessons in each classroom. We collected data for an average of 8.8 days in math classes and 8.1 days in social studies, reflecting the actual frequency with which the subjects were taught.

During each observation, one observer wrote open narrative notes on the activities and setting. The notes were subsequently rewritten on standard activity structure forms. The other observer collected data on the behavior of the eight sample students. Observers alternated in the two roles. The activity structure form and the individual student observation form are shown in appendix A.

The observer who recorded information about the activity structure noted the teacher's location, use of materials and behavior; student location and behavior; the materials in use; pacing of the lesson; content of the lesson; and the duration of various activities. The observer noted the location of children on classroom maps and recorded what was written on the blackboard. All of this information was used to determine the characteristics of activity segments.

As can be seen from perusing the activity structure form in appendix A, it would be difficult to physically reproduce an observer's entries here. However, two examples of the type and scope of information recorded in math classes will illustrate our method.

Ms. O.'s math class, located in an upper-middle-class suburb, was observed on Monday, April 27, from 9:33 to 10:30 A.M. Ms. O., eleven boys, and twelve girls were present.

Students were at their usual seats (see map) and the teacher was standing at the front of the room. At 9:33 she said, "Get ready for math," then arranged her own materials while students got out their homework papers and exchanged them with a classmate. At 9:36 Ms. O. started reading off answers to the homework assignment (p. 105 workbook for *Mathematics around Us*) in her usual lightning fashion (one answer per 2–3 seconds). At 9:38 Ms. O. walked around the class briefly answering questions students had about marking. After having students return papers to their owners, at 9:41 she went to her desk and called out students' names. Each pupil said how many problems he or she missed, and Ms. O. recorded the information in her record book.

As the checking work began at 9:36, four students (J, L, S, H) went to the back room adjoining the classroom and seated themselves around the octagonal table. They remained there until the end of the math period working on a packet of math dittoes and other materials collated by the teacher. These students worked at an individual rate through the materials. The unit, dealing with mixed numerals, is the same as that being studied by the rest of the class, but this advanced group demonstrated enough knowledge (through prior testing on the unit) to be given enrichment materials on the same topic—a policy followed in this district. The students solve their assigned problems, consult with one another when necessary, and go into the main room to check their answers from the teacher's edition, a procedure expected of all students in this classroom.

At 9:45 Ms. O. is at the blackboard in front of the room and says, "Today we'll do the same thing but a little bit different." There are groans from the class. Ms. O. sings out, "Don't gag and complain." She then starts to explain how to compare two mixed numbers with unlike denominators. At 9:49 she has students turn to page 291 in the textbook and asks students to do the first few examples on scratch paper. She goes around the room quickly looking at their work and then has nine students each do a problem (#13–21) on the blackboard as the other students watch, some getting restless and socializing. Ms. O. goes over each problem on the board, reinforcing and elaborating on her earlier instructions to compare the whole numbers first and then look at the fractional part.

At 10:03 Ms. O. writes the assignment on the blackboard (p. 106, show work, put in sign, circle largest; p. 295 LOWEST TERMS—a review to be done in preparation for test tomorrow). Students mainly stay at their desks and do the assigned problems. However, students get up to check their work in the teacher's edition of the textbook, and some go to the teacher's desk to ask questions. At 10:15, for example, in the main classroom the observer noted three students checking work, two at the teacher's desk, twelve in their desks working, and two out of the room. At 10:30 the teacher asked students to put their work away and the lesson ended.

Mrs. C.'s math class, located in a working-class suburb, was observed on Monday, February 5, from 1:03 to 1:54 P.M. The teacher, Mrs. C., thirteen boys and seven girls were present.

Students were at their usual seats (see map) while the teacher began the period standing by her desk and looking over her record book.

She spent three minutes in an organizational segment in which students found out who owed her papers and when they were due. She also told the whole class that today they were "going to do some work on fractions again" because they had not done it well last week, and then they were going to finish up the chapter review they had started on the previous Friday.

At 1:07 Mrs. C. goes to the blackboard, instructing students to look at page 200, #16 of their *Exploring Mathematics* textbook. She starts by asking students, "What is the numerator in $\frac{7}{8}$? What does it tell us?" Students respond when called on, and four students are asked in turn to go to the blackboard and draw illustrations of certain fractions such as $\frac{1}{4}$ and $\frac{2}{5}$ by shading appropriate portions of shapes. In the course of the lesson, Mrs. C. spontaneously generates some similar problems which she gives students to do at their desks on scratch paper and quickly walks around to check their work on these problems.

At 1:27 Mrs. C. hands back corrected pages of work students did on Friday (selected problems from the chapter review on page 193). She wants students to complete the assignment if necessary and to correct those problems she marked as incorrect. She lists all problems to be completed on the blackboard (e.g., 1–24, 29–36) and then answers questions from students about what to do first, etc. (We have a copy of each problem students are asked to solve.) Some students start working at their desks right away, while others raise procedural questions. At 1:31, somewhat exasperated, Mrs. C. says, "What are you to do first? Boy, this kills me! We've spent five minutes on directions." She then walks around to individual students' desks answering their questions, making comments on their work, and checking their progress. Occasionally she makes a comment meant to be heard by the whole class. Until 1:52 students work individually at their desks on their chapter review problems, some interact briefly with the teacher but rarely speak to one another. The observer comments that only one student seemed to be done before the period was over and he went to the reading table and read "The Starwars Storybook"—an accepted procedure when an assignment was completed. At 1:52 Mrs. C. said, "All right. Those finished, bring papers to me. Others will finish tomorrow. Get lined up." The class exited at 1:54.

While the first observer recorded information about classroom activities, the second observer sampled the behavior of the eight subjects in a fixed but random order, watching each pupil for five seconds and then writing a brief description of the student's behavior and coding task involvement. After thirty seconds, another student was observed. After two rotations of eight students each (eight minutes of observation) the observer took a one-minute break and then resumed.

DATA-CODING PROCEDURES

Identifying Segments

Every activity structure record was read in its entirety, and then T. Ferguson and I identified activity segments in each record. Segments were distinguished using the key characteristics in Gump's (1967) definition. Membership change, instructional format change, change of physical location, discontinuity of time, and change of instructional topics or materials all indicated that a new segment should be coded. Transitions were separated from instructional segments.[7]

In the example of Ms. O.'s math class, there were five segments. The first was a transition. The next two segments began simultaneously. Most class members were in a checking work activity, while four students pursued individualized seatwork for the remainder of the class period. After checking work, the students were in a recitation, followed by seatwork.

There were also five segments in Mrs. C.'s math lesson. In the order they occurred, their instructional formats were: giving instructions, recitation, giving instructions, seatwork, and transition.

Coding Segment Properties

For every instructional segment, we coded fifteen activity segment properties (or features), the kinds of materials used by students and teachers, the participants in the segment, and related information. The activity segment properties (introduced in the preceding chapter) included instructional format, expected student behavior pattern, pacing, options, expected student interaction, cognitive level, feedback, student location, and teacher leadership role. Definitions of the activity segment properties along with examples are in appendix B.[8] The reader is urged to examine the examples in appendix B to obtain a concrete understanding of the coding criteria and the classroom events that were quantified, which will be described in subsequent chapters.

Our examples can illustrate the coding. Segment 2 in Ms. O.'s lesson was checking work (instructional format) and teacher-paced (pacing), students were at their desks (location), and checking work (student behavior pattern). No student interaction (expected interaction) was permitted, students had no choice about doing the activity (options), and they were receiving information (cognitive level). The teacher, who was present and reading off answers (teacher role, feedback), used the teacher's edition of the textbook (materials used by teacher), while students used pencil and paper (materials used by students). Nineteen students were in the segment. Their participation did not depend on ability or interest. The segment lasted nine minutes and was simultaneous with one other segment.

Segment 3 in Ms. O.'s class was individualized seatwork (instructional format) in which four students, placed there by ability, participated. The teacher was not present (teacher role). The activity was student-paced (pacing), students were in a room adjoining the classroom (location), solving written problems (student behavior pattern). Students could interact with one another as needed (expected student interaction), worked through materials at their own rate (options), and were practicing skills and concepts (cognitive level). Students used a textbook, workbook, worksheets, paper, pencil, and the teacher's manual to check answers (materials used by students, feedback). The segment lasted fifty-four minutes.

In Mrs. C.'s class, segment 2 was a recitation (instructional format), led by the teacher (pacing, teacher role) directed toward concepts and skills (cognitive level), and had no student interaction (expected student interaction) or student choice of activity (options). Students solved problems at the blackboard and their desks (student behavior pattern) while using the textbook, paper and pencil, and the blackboard (materials used by students). The teacher used the teacher's edition of the textbook (materials used by teacher) to read off answers (feedback). Twenty students, not grouped by ability or interest, were in the segment, which lasted twenty minutes.

Coding Student Involvement

A student was deemed "on task" if during the observation interval he or she appeared to be actively engaged in an activity prescribed or permitted by the teacher. A student was coded "off task" if waiting, socializing, or daydreaming. If the observer could not judge whether the student was on or off task, a question mark was recorded. During training, field reliability standards were established by having two observers watch children simultaneously. Agreement levels of approximately 90 percent were achieved among pairs of observers.

DATA ANALYSIS

Interdependence in the Data

The main variables derived from the observations are segment properties and assessments of student involvement in activity segments. There is some lack of independence in estimates of student involvement because they are derived from multiple observations of the same students. There is also a lack of independence in segment features because data are pooled at the segment level but come in batches from classrooms. A variety of other factors also contribute to interdependence in the data.[9]

In general, the data we collected do not meet the assumptions of standard statistical procedures, although they are well suited for descriptive purposes. Consequently, testing for statistical significance was largely eschewed. However, standard statistical procedures were used to suggest the existence of relationships and to help organize and display data in ways familiar to readers. And in some instances, the data do conform to statistical assumptions. However, major emphasis was placed on data display and interpretation rather than testing for statistical significance levels.

BASIC DESCRIPTIVE INFORMATION ON THE OBSERVATIONAL DATA

Twenty math classes and nineteen social studies classes were observed. Twenty-one different teachers from eleven districts and thirteen schools participated. Fifteen teachers taught both math and

Table 2.2. Teacher Designation and Characteristics of Sample Classrooms

	Mathematics				Social Studies				
Teacher	Expenditure Level	SES	Self-Contained/ Departmentalized	Tracked	Teacher	Expenditure Level	SES	Self-Contained/ Departmentalized	Tracked
A	Low	Low	S-C	Yes	A	Low	Low	S-C	Yes
P	Low	Med	Dept	Yes	Q	Low	Med	Dept	Yes
P	Low	Med	Dept	Yes	Q	Low	Med	Dept	Yes
B	Low	Low	Dept	Yes	B	Low	Low	Dept	Yes
C	Low	Low	Dept	Yes	C	Low	Low	Dept	Yes
D	Low	Med	S-C	No	D	Low	Med	S-C	No
E	Low	Med	S-C	No	E	Low	Med	S-C	No
F	High	Low	S-C	No	F	High	Low	S-C	No
G	High	Low	S-C	No	G	High	Low	S-C	No
H	High	Low	S-C	No	H	High	Med	S-C	No
I	High	Med	S-C	No	I	High	Med	S-C	No
R	High	Med	S-C	No	T	High	High	Dept	Yes
S	High	High	Dept	Yes	J	High	High	Dept	No
J	High	High	Dept	No	K	High	Med	Dept	Yes
K	High	Med	Dept	Yes	U	High	Med	Dept	Yes
K	High	Med	Dept	Yes	L	High	High	S-C	No
L	High	High	Dept	Yes	M	High	High	S-C	No
M	High	High	Dept	Yes	N	High	High	S-C	No
N	High	High	Dept	Yes	O	High	High	S-C	No
O	High	High	S-C	No					

Note: See Table 2.1 for SES and Expenditure Level category definitions.

social studies. There were six teachers and twelve classes from low-SES schools, eight teachers and fifteen classes from medium-SES schools, and seven teachers and twelve classes from high-SES schools. Every teacher had at least three years' experience. Twenty-five classes were in high-expenditure districts, and fourteen classes were in low-expenditure districts.

Eleven math classes were departmentalized, while nine were self-contained. In social studies, eight classes were departmentalized, and eleven were self-contained. In all but one math and one social studies class, departmentalization and tracking by ability occurred together. In addition, one self-contained social studies class and one self-contained math class were tracked. Table 2.2 shows the characteristics of each sample classroom and identifies the individual teachers. The order of classes and teachers in table 2.2 is used in all tables and figures that contain data about individual classrooms.

The math data come from 7,804 minutes of observation over 176 days. The social studies classes were observed for a total of 6,649 minutes, 153 days. The average number of days of observation in a math class was 8.8 (SD = 1.1) and in a social studies class was 8.1 (SD = 1.6). Average length of a math class period was 44.2 minutes (SD = 7.0). Average length of social studies periods was 43.2 minutes (SD = 10.2). The average number of total minutes observed was 390.2 (SD = 84.3) in math classes and 350 (SD = 121.5) in social studies classes. The number of instructional segments, the number of instructional segments for which involvement estimates were available, and the length of time and number of class periods each class was observed are shown in table C.1 in appendix C.

After the data were coded, 708 math segments and 669 social studies segments were identified. Of the math segments, 173 were transitions and 535 were instructional. Similarly, of the social studies segments, 124 were transitions and 545 were instructional. The average number of instructional segments per math class period was 2.99 (SD = .82), and the average number of instructional social studies segments per class period was 3.61 (SD = 1.76). The average duration of instructional segments in math was 19.45 minutes (SD = 12.54), and in social studies it was 18.39 (SD = 12.23). An average transition segment lasted 4.73 minutes (SD = 4.41) in math and 4.77 minutes (SD = 4.44) in social studies.

3

Subject Matter Differences in Classroom Activity

This is the first of two chapters in which study results are presented. The main theme of this chapter is that there is considerable homogeneity in math instruction, whereas variety is characteristic of social studies instruction. Across math classes, uniformity is evident in the content of lessons, as well as in the forms of instruction, cognitive goals, and student behaviors. We found more diversity in topics, approaches, and goals both within and across social studies classes. By describing the features of the observed activity segments in detail, we provide the basis for noting similarities and differences in classroom activity in the two subjects.

LESSON TOPICS

An orientation to the math and social studies instruction we observed is provided by looking at the topics our pupils studied. In our description of curricula, we noted that fifth-grade math programs emphasize operations with whole numbers, fractions, and decimals—and that is what we saw.

The specific mathematics topics taught during our observations are shown in figure 3.1. Each row in the figure represents a class listed in the order in table 2.2, so it is possible to see the range of topics included in all classes, as well as the topics covered in a two-week period of instruction in each class.[1] Topics occur in a fairly standardized order. For example, basic operations (addition, subtraction, multiplication, and division) are taught in the stated sequence. Similarly, a class learning operations with fractions, mixed numbers, or decimals is likely to have had prior instruction in operations with whole numbers. We observed some variation in topics, since our observations took place between January and May. The progress of classes through the typical sequence also depended on the abilities of students and the nature of the school district.

Figure 3.1. Mathematics Topics by Class (*N* = 20)

Whole Numbers	Fractions	Mixed Numerals	Decimals	Geometry	Other
+ − × ÷	+ − EF				
+ − × ÷	+ − × C, R, CM				
+ − × ÷	+ − × C, R, CM				
+ − × ÷ E, F	+ − × R, CM, EF	CF		Perimeter	
+ − × ÷ A	R, CM, EF	Concept			Metrics
+ − ÷	+ × R, CM, EF	Concept			
+ − × ÷	+ × C, R, EF				
+ −	+ − × ÷				
				Line Segments, Angles, Polygons	Metrics
× ÷	+ − R	Concept			

+ × ÷	A	×	CD, CM, CP	CD, CF	CF, CM		Percent
	F	+	R, EF		CF, PV		Metrics
					+ − PV		Metrics
+ − × ÷	A	+ − × ÷	R, CM, EF	× ÷		Area, Perim., Vol., Polygons, Graphing	
* × ÷	E, F	× ÷	R, CM	+ −	+		Sets
* + − ÷	F	+ − ×		+ − × ÷		Line Segments, Hexagon	Roman Numerals
*		+ − × ÷	R, CM	×		Angles, Graphing	
* + − ÷	F	×	R, CM	CF	PV	Graphing	
		÷	R, CM	+			

Key: A = Averaging; R = Reducing; CP = Changing to percent; C = Canceling; CD = Changing to decimals; EF = Equivalent fractions; E = Estimating; CF = Changing to fractions; PV = Place value; F = Factoring; CM = Changing to mixed numerals. *Class used an individualized mathematics program. The topics indicated are based on the observations of project students; other topics might have been covered by other students.

As we expected after examining charts of textbook scope and sequence, our classroom data indicated considerable uniformity in topical coverage and sequence. It is virtually certain that an observer in fifth-grade math classes would see instruction relating to operations with mixed numbers, fractions, and decimals. In addition, the metric system, geometry, and numeration were covered in a few classes; the timing of their introduction, however, was not consistent across these classes.

As our overview of programs suggested, the content of social studies instruction is not nearly as uniform as that of math programs. Some children were learning United States or Latin American geography or history, others used *Man: A Course of Study (MACOS)*. We saw some pupils discussing family relationships and creating new societies, while others were making craft items related to different countries' traditions. Children also dealt with current events and studied careers.

Topics from the disciplines of history, geography, anthropology, economics, psychology, and civics were all taught to our fifth graders, but similarity across classes frequently stopped at the disciplinary level (see figure 3.2). For instance, while half the classes studied history, specific topics included Latin America, colonial America, ancient China, and the Civil War. A similar range was found in classes studying geography, culture, and economics.

It is important to look across the rows in figure 3.2 to see how many different topics appeared in a social studies class in a two-week observation period. Such an exercise illustrates that some of the classes had seemingly disjunctive curricula, while others were more unified. Some activities, such as reporting on current events, occurred on a regular basis and were not intended to be integrated with other study topics. But some classes seemed to jump from one topic to another in a confusing cafeteria style. In one class, for instance, students worked on the history of the old West and Rocky Mountain geography, Communism and its threat to the United States, moral dilemmas, and current events in a two-week interval. Other classes covered a variety of topics but in a coherent manner— for example, classes in which both the history and geography of Latin America were studied, or a class in which children learned about Arctic migration patterns, Eskimo society, and Eskimo division of labor.

A sequential ordering of topics is not usually found in social studies except when a historical or chronological order is used. The lack of sequential constraint is certainly one reason for the topical diversity we observed. The inclusion of so many subject fields under the umbrella of social studies is another. Jarolimek (1977) asserts that U.S. history, sometimes accompanied by study of Latin America and Canada, is the most prevalent social studies course for the fifth grade. Thirteen of our classes were covering topics that were part of the standard pattern, while the other six were studying regions outside the Americas (e. g., ancient China, Israel, the Arctic) or were not studying history or geography.

INSTRUCTIONAL ACTIVITY

While analysis of the topics of instruction is informative, in this work we are primarily concerned with the ingredients of classroom activity. The math lesson in Ms. O.'s class, described in chapter 2, contained almost every form of instructional activity used regularly in the math classes we saw. Mostly, students had a steady diet: checking work, recitations, and seatwork with either uniform or individual assignments. Only an occasional contest, game, or test broke the predictable math regimen.

In general, social studies lessons were not as predictable and consistent as math classes. We found more diversity in a given social studies class from day to day and more variety in instructional approach from class to class. Some short descriptions of actual lessons illustrate typical social studies experiences and complement the descriptions of math lessons given previously.

Mr. Q.'s class in a working-class town had a traditional curriculum focused on geography and history. When we observed the group of twenty-six, they were studying Latin America.

During one observation period, Mr. Q.'s class spent five minutes to complete a film strip on rubber production which they had started the day before. Students took turns reading the captions. After the filmstrip, students opened their workbooks in order to correct the previous night's homework. Mr. Q. read off answers to questions about South America and discussed alternatives with students. Eventually, students tallied their scores and turned in their workbooks.

During the remaining 17 minutes of the period, students worked with a dictionary to define a list of terms including "Creole," "import," "sombrero," and "grove." Students

Figure 3.2. Social Studies Topics by Class ($N = 19$)

Format[a]	History	Geography	Society/ Culture	Economics	Civics	Psychology	Careers	Current Events
G					Purpose of Rules			•
T	Latin American	Latin American						
T	Latin American	Latin American						
T	Colonial							
T	Colonial	Colonial						
T			Industrialization				•	

T		U.S.	Aztecs, Modern American		•	
G	Old West	Rocky Mountain		Communism		•
T	Civil War	U.S.		Moral Dilemmas		•
T	Pacific U.S.	Pacific U.S.	Inventions	Pacific Natural Resources, Industry		
T		Pacific U.S.				
G			Israel			
M	Ancient China			Stock Market		•
G	Settling New World (Simulation)		Colonial			

(continued)

Figure 3.2. (Continued)

Format[a]	History	Geography	Society/Culture	Economics	Civics	Psychology	Careers	Current Events
M	A. Lincoln	N. & S. America				Family Problems		
G			Eskimos	Natural Resources				
G		Arctic Migration	Eskimos	Eskimo Division of Labor, Natural Resources			•	
T	Colonial, Civil War							
M		U.S.		Taxes, Profit, Supply-demand	Federal, State, Local Govts.			

[a]T = teacher-centered; G = group work; M = mixed format.

were permitted to go to the teacher's desk to ask him questions, and many did. Otherwise students worked individually at their desks, writing definitions as they obtained them.

On our next day of observation, Mr. Q.'s class had an orally administered true-false test with questions about South America (19 minutes) and then corrected it under the teacher's supervision (13 minutes). For the last 11 minutes of the period, there was a contest in which two students went to the blackboard and wrote as many two-syllable words as they could in one minute. Pairs of students, each representing a team, took turns at the board. There was no discernible connection between the game and the curricular content.

Another version of social studies characterized by a lot of instructional variety was evident in Ms. O.'s class. The class was composed of the same twenty-three youngsters we observed under Ms. O.'s tutelage for math.

On one day the class began with a 14-minute recitation in which students discussed the services that are provided by people in different occupations. The recitation was in conjunction with a reading section from their textbook, *Social Sciences: Concepts and Values.*

After a short explanation of how to proceed, students completed a seatwork assignment in the workbook that accompanies their textbook for the remainder of the period. The assignment was difficult, dealing with profit and loss, and the teacher circulated to assist students continuously.

On another day in Ms. O.'s class, students took a test, corrected the test, and then went to the resource center to do research for reports about individual states. In the resource center students used encyclopedias, atlases, and other books. The reports were done both individually and in groups.

On a subsequent day, students in Ms. O.'s class played a game involving naming and locating states on maps and listened to a number of students report on their state projects.

Mr. Q.'s and Ms. O.'s classes each experienced variety in social studies almost daily. In contrast, Mrs. K.'s class, which we describe next, had a more predictable activity structure than most social studies classes.

Mrs. K.'s class in a middle-class suburban school had fifteen students who were using a curriculum in which they were simulating colonizing a new world. The class divided into work groups almost every day we observed. The day described below was characteristic of the students' experience in Mrs. K.'s class.

As an observed lesson started, Mrs. K. explained that each group would have to decide on shipping supplies and other aspects of their sailing plans as outlined in a number of sheets they were to complete. After five minutes of general introduction, Mrs. K. directed the three work groups to different locations in the room. For the remaining 40 minutes, two groups of five girls and one group of five boys decided how many colonists would sail and completed a list of supplies to take on their ships. The whole exercise was structured with a set of rules governing what could be loaded on each ship. In a delightful episode, the boys' group decided to send nineteen men to the colony. One member asked how many women to send and another replied, "None. They'll waste our food. Why do we need women?" The recorder for the group said, "Otherwise our colony will die out. We need kids." Apparently unpersuaded, the group dropped the topic of women, and a member asked how many pigs they should take along. This suggestion also created problems because one of the boys said he couldn't eat pork and they shouldn't take pigs. They decided on fowl instead.

Segment Feature Measures

Throughout this chapter we will present data about the distributions of such segment features as instructional format and pacing. We will also show the average duration of different categories of segments. For every segment feature there are a number of mutually exclusive categories, one of which applied to every segment. Instructional format, for instance, had eighteen categories, while pacing had four. Because segments vary in duration and may include the entire class or a subset of students, two measures, which provide different but complementary information, are needed to provide a complete picture of the way a given segment feature is distributed: segment distributions and occupancy time distributions. Segment distributions give equal weight to every activity segment. Occupancy time is derived by multiplying segment duration by the number of students in the segment.

Let us take a simple example in which 10 pupils in a classroom are observed for 10 minutes. During the first 5 minutes all pupils take part in a recitation segment. During the next 5 minutes, 3 children are in a group working together, while the other 7 pupils do seatwork. Three activity segments, with a total of 100 pupil minutes (10 pupils × 10 minutes), are found in this example. If we are interested in the feature instructional format, we calculate both a segment distribution and an occupancy time distribution for instructional format. The segment distribution shows that three segments occurred—one each of recitation, group work, and seatwork. Thus, each of these instructional format categories accounted for one-third of the segments. In terms of occupancy time, however, recitation took 50 pupil minutes (10 pupils × 5 minutes), group work took 15 pupil minutes (3 pupils × 5 minutes), and seatwork took 35 pupil minutes (7 pupils × 5 minutes). Since there were 100 pupil minutes in all, 50 percent (50/100 pupil minutes) of occupancy time was spent in recitation, 15 percent in group work, and 35 percent in seatwork.

Occupancy time distributions and segment distributions are similar when most activities are whole-class segments involving all pupils. The two measures diverge when there are simultaneous segments in which subsets of pupils are involved or segments of markedly different durations. Occupancy time distributions reflect pupil time allocations, so they are a good indication of how a child spends his or her time through the period observed. Segment distributions are more closely related to the way in which teachers plan and conduct the instructional period in terms of the activities of all children. In our example, an average pupil will spend half the time in recitation, but only 15 percent of class time in group work. The teacher, however, has planned and conducted three segments, two of which are simultaneous.

Instructional Formats

We turn now to a detailed look at the activity segment features in the two subject areas. Instructional format is the most general characterization of activity segments. The codes include well-established descriptors of major patterns of instruction, such as recitation, seatwork, and lecture. In the social studies examples, Mr. Q.'s class participated in segments with film (audiovisual), checking work, seatwork, test, and contest formats. Ms. O.'s pupils were members of segments with recitation, seatwork, test, contest, and student report formats. The students in Mrs. K.'s class, on the other hand, participated in segments with only two instructional formats: task preparation and group work. In the math examples in chapter 2, Ms. O.'s pupils participated in checking work, recitation, individualized seatwork, and uniform seatwork. In Mrs. C.'s class, pupils were involved in recitation, giving instructions, and uniform seatwork.

In mathematics, all forms of seatwork (uniform seatwork, diverse seatwork, and individualized seatwork) together accounted for about 40 percent of the segments observed. Uniform seatwork (frequently referred to simply as seatwork) is coded when the whole class is doing the same assignment. Diverse seatwork occurs when pupils are working on a variety of tasks, and individualized seatwork signifies that pupils are working at their own rate through a sequence of tasks. Twenty-nine percent of math instructional segments were recitations. Checking work and contests (or games) each accounted for about 8 percent of the math segments. Other formats—such as giving instructions, tests, and lectures—occurred very infrequently.

As the data in table 3.1 show, the segment and occupancy time distributions were very similar for the math segments because frequently occurring instructional format categories involved the whole class and were of relatively similar durations. Table C.2 in appendix C shows the durations of math and social segments by instructional format and other segment features. Seatwork segments, particularly individualized ones, were longer than other math segments, such as recitations or checking work.

The formats in social studies were distributed differently than those in math. Seatwork and recitation each constituted 18 percent of the segments, while 34 percent consisted of group work, in which children formed face-to-face groups. Giving instructions, a format that often precedes small-group work, accounted for about 8 percent. Discussions, student reports, and film/audiovisual segments each made up about 4 percent of the social studies segments.

In social studies, comparing proportions of segments with proportions of occupancy time resulted in noticeable differences. Since occupancy time weights segment durations by the number of pupils in the segment, small groups or part-class segments reduce occupancy time proportions in those formats in which they occur. While about a third of the social studies segments were group work, students spent only about 11 percent of their time in them. On the

Table 3.1. Distributions of Instructional Formats

	Mathematics			Social Studies		
Format	N	Segments (%)	Occupancy Time (%)	N	Segments (%)	Occupancy Time (%)
Uniform seatwork	144	26.9	29.8	69	12.7	21.8
Individualized seatwork	59	11.0	13.7	—	—	—
Diverse seatwork	14	2.6	3.8	26	4.8	6.1
Recitation	155	28.9	30.9	96	17.6	28.1
Group work	1	0.2	0.1	183	33.6	10.7
Contest, game	44	8.2	6.2	8	1.5	1.5
Checking work	42	7.8	5.9	12	2.2	2.4
Giving instructions/ task preparation	33	6.2	1.7	58	10.9	5.4
Student reports	—	—	—	20	3.7	6.9
Discussion	2	0.4	0.4	19	3.5	3.1
Test	18	3.4	5.1	10	1.8	3.9
Lecture/demonstration	15	2.8	1.9	12	2.2	2.5
Film/audiovisual	—	—	—	24	4.4	6.8
Tutorial	8	1.5	0.2	—	—	—
Stocks	—	—	—	8	1.5	0.8
Total instructional segments	535	100.0	100.0	545	100.0	100.0

other hand, about 28 percent of student time was spent in seatwork, and another 28 percent was in recitations; these formats almost always involved all class members. Similarly, film/audiovisual and student report segments each took about 7 percent of students' time.

Certain formats were found only in one subject or the other. Peculiar to math were individualized seatwork and the infrequently occurring tutorial. Used in social studies but not math were student reports, small-group work, film/audiovisual, and stock market studies.[2]

Within the entire collection of segments, a greater variety of formats was used in social studies than in math. To discover whether there was also more variety in format use within a given social studies class than a given math class, we averaged the number of formats used in all social studies and math classes, respectively. The mean number of formats used in social studies classes (7.16; SD = 2.11) was significantly higher than the mean number of formats used in math classes (5.8; SD = 2.09) according to a t-test ($t = 2.04$, $p < .05$).

In social studies, variety in topics and curricular approaches occurred from school to school and extended to individual teachers who tended to use more formats for instruction. In math, the dominant formats (defined as those that occupy at least 19 percent of student time) were recitations, the seatwork varieties, and contests. Seatwork and recitation also occurred frequently in social studies, but group work, films, and student reports were dominant formats in some classes.

While the multifarious nature of social studies classes is clear with respect to topical coverage and instructional format, an examination of other segment features is needed to round out the picture. Among others, student behavior pattern, pacing, expected student interaction, cognitive goals, and feedback will be looked at in turn.

Student Behavior Patterns

Twenty-eight possible categories of student behavior were distinguished, and the main expected behavioral pattern was coded for every segment. The segment and occupancy time distributions of student behavior patterns occupying at least 1 percent of student time or accounting for 1 percent of the segments in each subject area are given in table 3.2. Behaviors are listed for each subject in descending order according to the proportion of segments in which they occurred.

Two features convey the main story. Many fewer behavior patterns occurred in the math than in social studies segments, and the distribution of occupancy times was distinct in the two areas. In math, one behavior pattern—solving problems at one's desk—accounted for over half the student time. In addition, students answered and asked questions, solved problems at the blackboard, watched others solve problems at the blackboard, checked work, and took tests. In social studies, more behavior patterns were observed, and student time was spread much more evenly across

Table 3.2. Distributions of Student Behavior Patterns

Behavior Pattern[a]	N	Segments (%)	Occupancy Time (%)
		Mathematics	
Solve/Desk	224	41.87	51.40
Question/Answer	55	10.28	9.13
Blackboard/Watch[b]	46	8.60	8.66
Checking Work	40	7.48	5.59
Listening	39	7.29	2.79
Game—Cognitive	31	5.79	3.15
Blackboard/Solve[b]	29	5.42	6.87
Test	19	3.55	5.43
Choral[b]	8	1.50	1.46
Tutor[b]	8	1.50	0.25
Q/A—Oral Reading	7	1.31	0.88
Read/Oral	4	0.75	1.24
Other (<1%)	25	4.67	3.14
Total	535	100.01	99.99
		Social Studies	
Listening	72	13.21	10.43
Discuss/Listen[b]	52	9.54	6.41
Question/Answer	47	8.62	9.67
Q/A—Oral Reading	42	7.71	13.31
Research[b]	38	6.97	6.84
Solve/Desk	37	6.79	5.53
Game—Cognitive	36	6.61	1.66
Write[b]	30	5.50	3.78
Crafts[b]	27	4.95	3.02
Variety[b]	26	4.77	5.00
Maps[b]	23	4.22	7.67
Film/AV[b]	23	4.22	6.49
Drawing/Painting[b]	22	4.04	2.54
Checking Work	12	2.20	2.42
Graphs[b]	12	2.20	2.09
Test	10	1.83	3.94
Read/Oral	8	1.47	4.94
Rehearse Play[b]	6	1.10	0.43
Read/Silent[b]	5	0.92	1.43
Other (<1%)	17	3.12	2.42
Total	545	99.99	100.02

[a]Behavior patterns are defined in appendix B.
[b]Behavior pattern occurs only in the designated subject area.

Table 3.3. Number of Behavior Patterns and Names of Dominant Behavior Patterns by Class

Mathematics Classes (N = 20)		Social Studies Classes (N = 19)	
No. Bhvrs	Dominant Behaviors[a]	No. Bhvrs	Dominant Behaviors[a]
* 8	Solve/Desk (59)	4	Discuss/Listen (46), Variety (43)
6	Solve/Desk (33), Blackboard/Solve (21), Black-board/Watch (19)	11	Research (27)
		12	Research (21)
8	Solve/Desk (19), Blackboard/Solve (26)	6	Q/A—Oral Reading (25), Q/A (23), Maps (21)
* 6	Solve/Desk (58), Blackboard/Watch (22)	7	Q/A (33), Write (26)
* 4	Solve/Desk (61), Q/A (22)	8	Q/A—Oral Reading (20), Listening (21)
*10	Solve/Desk (44)	15	Q/A—Oral Reading (29), Maps (20)
* 6	Solve/Desk (56), Q/A (21)	8	Draw-Paint (43)
* 8	Solve/Desk (24), Blackboard/Watch (29), Test (24)	9	Q/A—Oral Reading (35), Q/A (24)

* 6	Solve/Desk (63)	6	Read/Oral (51)
* 6	Solve/Desk (45), Choral (30)	6	Q/A—Oral Reading (46), Maps (42)
* 6	Solve/Desk (84)		
10	Solve/Desk (22), Blackboard/Watch (20)	6	Crafts (66)
9	Solve/Desk (40)	10	Discuss/Listen (31), Test (19)
* 5	Solve/Desk (57), Q/A (23)	9	Discuss/Listen (35), Listening (28)
* 2	Solve/Desk (80), Game—Cognitive (20)	11	Listening (24)
2	Solve/Desk (78), Game—Cognitive (22)	8	Game—Cognitive (21)
* 5	Solve/Desk (88)	11	Listening (20), Film/AV (22)
* 7	Solve/Desk (67)	10	Q/A (21), Research (21), Film/AV (19)
* 7	Solve/Desk (31), Q/A (25), Checking Work (20)	10	Q/A (27), Listening (22)
* 7	Solve/Desk (49), Checking Work (20)		
$\overline{X}$ 6.4		8.8	
S.D. 2.2		2.7	

aDominant behaviors occupy at least 19 percent of occupancy time. Percent of occupancy time is shown next to behavior name. Behaviors are defined in appendix B.
*Same teacher taught mathematics and social studies classes shown on same row.

them. The most frequently occurring pattern was answering and asking questions in the context of oral reading (13 percent occupancy time), followed by listening, and answering and asking questions—each of which occupied about 10 percent of student time. Eleven of the twenty behavior patterns seen in social studies were unique to the subject. The analogous number was four for mathematics.

Was the greater variation in social studies a product of the many curricula used? Were the behavior patterns within social studies classes varied, or were they simply different in different classes? Indeed, were the behavior patterns relatively unchanging in individual math classes?

The number of student behavior patterns observed in each class, and the names of the dominant behavior patterns (those with more than 19 percent occupancy time) along with their actual occupancy times are given in table 3.3. Each row in table 3.3 represents a separate class, listed in the order used in table 2.2. The teachers who taught both math and social studies are identified. The average number of behaviors per social studies class is significantly higher than that in math according to a t-test ($t = 3.07$; $p < .01$). The behaviors and their occupancy times reveal a remarkable uniformity in the math classes. Students solving problems at their desks was a dominant behavior in every class, with occupancy times ranging from 19 to 88 percent. Altogether eight different behavior patterns were dominant in math classes, including answering questions, watching problems being solved on the board, checking work, and taking tests.

Fourteen different behavior patterns were dominant in social studies classes, and no one behavior was found in class after class, as solving problems at one's desk was in math. Some of the diversity in social studies is attributable to very different behavioral patterns in different classrooms. We observed classes in which students spend a noticeable amount of their time doing research, participating in discussions, answering questions in the context of oral reading, watching films, working with maps, and listening, as well as other behaviors. Social studies classes were both more distinct from one another and internally more varied than math classes.

Materials

The materials used for instruction by each class are displayed in figure 3.3. The classes are listed in the order established in table 2.2. In the math classes, textbooks, workbooks, and worksheets are pervasive. Games, audiovisual materials (tape recorders for lessons), manipulatives, and reference books were each found in a minority of the math classes. About half the math classes had at least one of these types of materials in addition to texts and worksheets. Seven classes used only texts or worksheets. While the quality and type of texts, workbooks, and worksheets differed, children's range of experiences with instructional materials was restricted—another demonstration of the rather changeless quality of math settings.

In social studies, pupils encountered more types of materials. Textbooks and worksheets were used in about two-thirds of the classes. Audiovisual materials, maps, globes, and reference books were also common. Newspapers and magazines (usually weekly magazines produced for school use), craft materials, manipulatives, and games were also found in some classes. We also saw some unusual materials, such as an Aztec stone and a parchment replica of colonial documents. From the children's point of view, daily experiences in social studies were more varied with respect to the materials used, the behaviors expected, and the topics studied.

Pacing and Expected Social Interaction

Pacing is an assessment of who is actually setting the rate of work or activity in a given segment.[3] Educational conditions are often classified by whether children work on their own, with other pupils, or in direct interaction with the teacher. Different views of teaching and learning are frequently revealed in classrooms in which pacing opportunities are unalike.

We coded four categories of pacing: child, teacher, cooperative (child-child), and mechanical. Figure 3.4 shows both the segment and occupancy time distributions for pacing. It is interesting that the teachers actively directed classroom activities about half the time in both subjects but apportioned the remaining class time differently. In social studies there was more cooperative pacing and the only use of mechanical pacing; children worked on their own over half the time in math but less than one fourth the time in social studies.

Expected social interaction among students is closely related to pacing although not identical to it; such interaction was coded into four categories: none, low, medium, and high. Low was coded when infrequent work-related interactions were allowed. Medium interaction was coded for segments in which some children were working together and others worked alone. High interaction was coded when children were expected to work together.

Figure 3.3. Materials Used in Mathematics (*N* = 20) and Social Studies (*N* = 19) Classes

	Mathematics							Social Studies									
	Txbk/ Wkbk	Wk Shts	AV	Game	Ref Bks	News Mags	Manip	Txbk/ Wkbk	Wk Shts	AV	Game	Ref Bks	News Mags	Manip	Globe/ Maps	Craft Matl	Other
*	•								•					•		•	
	•	•		•					•	•		•	•		•		
	•	•		•					•	•		•			•		
*	•	•	•				•		•	•		•		•	•		•
*	•	•							•			•			•		
*	•	•				•			•	•		•			•	•	
*	•	•		•			•		•				•		•	•	•
*								•	•	•			•		•	•	
*					•			•					•				

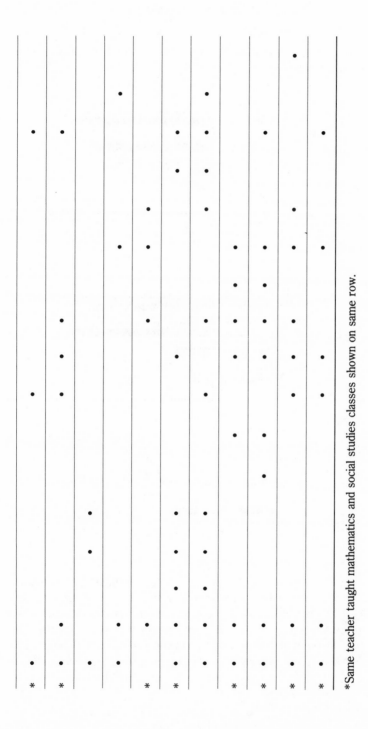

*Same teacher taught mathematics and social studies classes shown on same row.

Figure 3.4. Pacing Distributions in Mathematics and Social Studies Segments

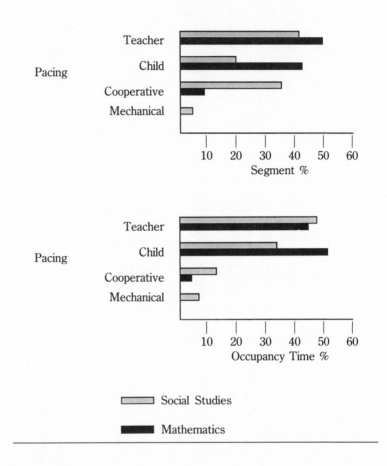

In both subjects students worked primarily under conditions in which they were not expected to interact with one another (table 3.4), but social studies had more segments in which interaction was either permitted or required. Some interaction was expected in about 20 percent of the math segments and in 47 percent of the social studies segments. In terms of actual student time, however, only 7 percent in math was truly interactive (medium or high); the comparable figure in social studies was 16 percent.

When we examined pacing and expected social interaction together, we found more interaction permitted in child-paced segments in social studies than in math. There was also a weaker trend of the same type under teacher pacing.[4] With only a few exceptions, cooperative pacing in both subjects co-occurred with either medium or high interaction.

Peer work groups in many social studies classes accounted for the greater degree of student interaction in the subject. Peer work groups are face-to-face groups that do not include the whole class and in which students are expected to interact without the teacher present (Graybeal and Stodolsky 1985). Overall, students were more than twice as likely to participate in a peer work group in social studies than in math. Across all classes, about 12 percent of student time in social studies and 5 percent in math was spent in peer work groups. However, only about half the classes in both subjects had these small-group experiences.

Elsewhere (Graybeal and Stodolsky 1985) we have presented a detailed analysis of the peer work groups observed in math and social studies. The quality of the activities and interactions in the groups was very distinct in the two subjects. Social studies peer work groups required a wide array of student behaviors including discussion, writing, research, crafts and art work, use and creation of maps, and cognitive games. Ninety percent of social studies peer work groups were fully cooperative—all members were expected to contribute and their efforts were evaluated as a group product. In math the peer work groups engaged primarily in games and contests or were involved in seatwork in which students helped one another. There were no groups in math in which students worked toward a common goal that was evaluated as a joint product.

The general lack of social interaction between children in our classrooms may not surprise the reader, but it is worthy of some reflection. In principle, children can facilitate cognitive learning for one another and meet each others' interpersonal and social needs. Teachers probably recognize the extent to which ten-year-old children are socially motivated and concerned. However, they seldom use peer interaction to support learning. Rather, social interests are often seen as a potential diversion from learning. Herbert Wright (1967) once described the relationships between

Table 3.4. Distributions of Segment Features

Segment Feature[a]	Mathematics			Social Studies		
	N	Segments (%)	Occupancy Time (%)	N	Segments (%)	Occupancy Time (%)
Pacing:						
Teacher	264	49.4	44.7	225	41.3	47.5
Child	226	42.2	51.2	106	19.5	33.5
Cooperative	45	8.4	4.1	191	35.1	12.5
Mechanical	—	—	—	23	4.2	6.5
Expected student interaction:						
None	429	80.3	82.8	291	53.4	72.9
Low	42	7.9	10.2	50	9.2	11.3
Medium	40	7.5	5.2	110	20.2	8.4
High	23	4.3	1.7	94	17.3	7.4
Task options:						
Teacher–Task and Time	445	83.2	80.4	440	80.7	84.0
Teacher–Task; Student–Time	6	1.1	1.2	1	0.2	0.2
Student–Task and Time	8	1.5	1.3	20	3.7	2.8
Student–Task; Teacher–Time	6	1.1	0.5	44	8.1	3.9
Teacher–Task and Time; Student–Material	2	0.4	0.1	36	6.6	8.0
Teacher–Task and Time; Student–Order	9	1.7	2.8	4	0.7	1.2
Individualized Program	59	11.0	13.7	—	—	—
Student location:						
Desks	358	66.9	69.9	396	72.7	78.4
Blackboard/Desks	78	14.6	15.8	—	—	—
Office	40	7.5	3.1	—	—	—
Work Area	22	4.1	6.8	39	7.2	7.0
Work Tables	—	—	—	19	3.5	1.6
Rug	—	—	—	14	2.6	1.2

Table 3.4. (*Continued*)

Segment Feature[a]	Mathematics			Social Studies		
	N	Seg- ments (%)	Occu- pancy Time (%)	N	Seg- ments (%)	Occu- pancy Time (%)
Student location, *cont.*						
Established Area[b]	—	—	—	19	3.5	3.6
Library	—	—	—	18	3.3	5.0
Resource Center	6	1.1	1.4	—	—	—
Other (<1%)	31	5.8	3.0	40	7.3	3.2
Feedback:						
Teacher–Low	144	27.0	28.3	187	34.3	32.9
Teacher–High	61	11.4	13.0	21	3.9	4.6
None	75	14.0	12.5	35	6.4	7.0
Student Feedback	39	7.3	3.3	81	14.9	7.4
Textbook Only	41	7.7	8.6	14	2.6	3.2
Not Applicable	20	3.8	1.0	55	10.1	8.9
Additional materials:						
Manipulatives	30	5.6	2.3	4	0.7	0.9
Books	1	0.2	—	32	5.9	4.1
Self-Check	19	3.6	2.7	3	0.6	0.7
Teacher–Low and Textbook	58	10.9	13.5	59	10.8	20.6
Teacher–Low and Additional Materials	21	3.9	7.9	48	8.8	8.3
Teacher–High and Additional Materials	25	4.7	7.0	6	1.1	1.4
Cognitive level:						
Not Cognitive	—	—	—	46	8.4	5.4
Receive/Recall Facts	90	16.9	10.3	182	33.4	36.5
Concepts and Skills	428	80.0	86.5	92	16.9	23.2
Research Skills A: Locate Information	—	—	—	36	6.6	6.6
Research Skills B: Symbolic/Graphic	—	—	—	51	9.4	13.8

(*continued*)

Table 3.4. (*Continued*)

		Mathematics			Social Studies	
Segment Feature[a]	N	Seg-ments (%)	Occu-pancy Time (%)	N	Seg-ments (%)	Occu-pancy Time (%)
Research Skills B, *cont.*						
Application	15	2.8	2.8	87	16.0	8.5
Other Higher Mental Processes	1	0.2	0.2	51	9.4	6.2
Teacher role:						
Watcher/Helper– Intermittent	159	29.7	34.2	252	46.2	35.0
Watcher/Helper– Continuous	26	4.9	8.1	11	2.0	3.1
Recitation Leader	171	32.0	32.7	130	23.9	33.8
Not in Segment	73	13.6	10.1	21	3.9	2.2
Action Director	45	8.4	6.1	71	13.0	14.8
Instructor	27	5.1	2.4	40	7.3	5.4
Reader	21	3.9	2.9	12	2.2	1.9
Tester	13	2.4	3.5	8	1.5	3.8

[a]Features are defined in appendix B.
[b]Students are working in an area set up specifically for the activity in which they are engaged.

parents and children in Midwest, a small town he studied intensively, as "a benevolent autocracy," an apt characterization of the classrooms we saw as well. Teachers appear to assume that a tight rein is needed in working with youngsters of this age.

Options

The teacher's control of classroom activity is strongly evident in the options children have in classrooms (see table 3.4). We found teacher-dominated programs, in which over 80 percent of both math and social studies segments involved tasks specified by the teacher. The teacher assigned the actual task and the time during which to do it. When students did individualized seatwork in math, they sometimes had a choice about the materials to use to attain their assigned learning goal. Otherwise, only 3 percent of the math segments involved any student choice of tasks. In social studies, students were more frequently given a choice of tasks (12 percent of segments) or materials in the context of a teacher-specified task (7 percent of segments). By and large, the students had very limited opportunities to choose either what they were working on or how they were to learn something.

Options often distinguish student-centered from teacher-centered approaches, and our classes were almost all teacher-centered. In ten math and ten social studies classes, all tasks were teacher-specified. Children could occasionally select material to use for an assignment in three social studies and in six math classes. In six social studies classes and four math classes, children selected tasks at least occasionally. There was only one school, characterized by a more open and student-centered orientation, in which students in both subjects spent the majority of their time in self-selected activity.

Child decision making, at least with regard to activities, was not a feature of the schools we studied. We found 80 percent of the math segments and 85 percent of the social studies segments had no options for children even when they finished work. In many classes, children were expected to wait quietly if they completed work ahead of other pupils. In some classes, pupils could do subject-related work or complete any unfinished work. Occasionally children were also permitted to read.

Location and Time of Day

Student location (table 3.4) also reflects the generally formal character of the classrooms we observed. Students were at their desks at least two-thirds of the time in both subjects. In math, most of their remaining time was spent at the blackboard. In social studies, students were never at the blackboard but were in a variety of other locations such as work areas, the library, and on rugs.

Weiss (1978) demonstrated that more time is allocated to basic subjects such as math than to enrichment fields like social studies. Our findings were similar. We also looked at when each subject was taught in the school day. In our schools, math was taught during periods thought most conducive to learning—mornings or directly after lunch. With a handful of exceptions, math was taught before social studies in the daily schedule.

Feedback

Feedback refers to ways in which students can gain information about the correctness of their performance, get help in accomplishing a task, or both. In fifth grade, feedback about correctness of performance is often delayed—most commonly when children submit written work to the teacher and it is corrected and returned later. But feedback can also occur during class periods. As Grannis (1978) suggests, feedback is probably most important when children are working on their own, as in the typical seatwork situation.

Most types of feedback are used in both math and social studies classes (table 3.4). When feedback is available, the teacher can be the only source, students can have access to information from the materials they use, or both materials and the teacher can provide feedback in a given segment. In both fields, the teacher (with or without materials) provides help or feedback to students about two-thirds of the time. Common settings for teacher feedback are recitations, discussions, checking work, and seatwork in which students are completing problem sets and other written assignments.

The distribution of feedback categories differed somewhat for the two subjects, partly reflecting the relatively greater proportion of student time in child-paced settings in math and cooperative settings in social studies. In math, students spent more time with no feedback available, or under conditions in which teachers provided high levels of feedback by intensively interacting with or supervising them. Textbooks and manipulatives served as the sole sources of feedback more often in math than in social studies.[5] On the other hand, children in social studies classes were more frequently under low levels of teacher supervision, gave one another feedback more often, and used books (not textbooks) as information sources more frequently. Social studies students also participated in a larger proportion of segments in which feedback was not applicable, such as watching films. The data suggest that students may regularly use more sources of feedback and information in addition to the teacher in social studies than in math—an important point to which we will return in our discussion of routes to learning in chapter 5.

Cognitive Level

We have been describing the conditions under which students work, but now we ask the crucial questions: What intellectual processes are students asked to perform? What learning objectives are sought in the activity segments we have been describing? We coded each segment for the cognitive processes inferred to be the goal of the instructional task or activity. Thus coding required making a judgment about the major intellectual purpose of each segment.

The coding is essentially a modification of the *Taxonomy of Educational Objectives* (Bloom et al. 1956) and incorporates some ideas from Orlandi (1971), who discusses objectives in social studies curricula. Our system is partially hierarchical, collapsing the six levels in the *Taxonomy* to four categories: receiving and recalling information (level one); learning concepts and skills and comprehension (level two); application of concepts and skills (level three); and other higher mental processes (levels four to six). The two lowest levels are less cognitively complex than the others.

Two categories dealing with research skills in social studies were also defined. These categories encompass a variety of levels of complexity but are at least level two. "Research skills A: location of information" is often centered around obtaining and comprehending information, as well as actually practicing reference tool skills. The students in Ms. O.'s class collecting information for their state reports were working at this level. "Research skills B: use and interpretation of symbolic and graphic data" includes instances in which students read and acquire skills to read maps, graphs, charts, tables, and cartoons. They also learn to display information in such pictorial or graphic forms as maps, charts, and graphs.

In addition to the six categories discussed, we occasionally found a segment that seemed to have no cognitive goal, either because the activity emphasized social or affective processes or because the tasks were so low-level as to represent no real opportunity for cognitive learning. Such segments were coded "not cognitive."

The categories form an approximate—not a strict—hierarchy of five levels in terms of complexity—the dimension underlying the original *Taxonomy*. "Not cognitive" segments are the lowest, followed respectively by "receiving or recalling facts," "learning concepts and skills," and "research skills A and B," which range from the preceding level upward. "Application" and "other higher mental processes" are considered similar in complexity and are at the top of the ordering.

What is the distribution of cognitive levels found in the activity segments we observed? Table 3.4 shows the distribution of cognitive levels ordered by complexity. Math segments are overwhelmingly directed to the learning of concepts, skills, and algorithms (level two of the *Taxonomy*). As we saw in the topical analysis, most segments entail learning operations with whole numbers, fractions, and decimals, and they emphasize the mastery of algorithms and specific numerical routines. Seventeen percent of the segments in math are at the low level of receiving/recalling facts. Many of these segments consist of checking answers. Three percent of the segments involve application, the only higher mental activity coded in the math classes. Application typically occurs when students use an algorithm to solve a word problem. We may have slightly underestimated the actual extent of application in the math classes by only coding the major intellectual process in each segment. If one or two word problems were part of a longer algorithmically oriented segment, application would not have been coded as the main intellectual goal. However, even if an underestimation occurred, there is no doubt that the amount of application activity in the math classes was minimal.

In social studies we found much more variety in cognitive goals. There was considerable emphasis on the acquisition of facts and information at a lower mental process level, but higher mental processes and research skills were also goals of instruction. About a third of student time was spent on facts, commonly when students were answering questions or listening to reports. About 23 percent of student time was devoted to attaining concepts and skills and comprehension activities. Research skills, using reference books, maps, charts, and graphs, occupied another 23 percent of student time. About 15 percent was directed toward application and other higher mental processes. Additionally, 5 percent of student time in social studies was spent on tasks that did not have a discernible cognitive goal.

In the next chapter, we will examine in detail the contexts in which pupils pursue different cognitive goals. Here is suffices to note that, in contrast to math, social studies programs required more diverse intellectual processes, and the variation in cognitive goals occurred within as well as across classes. Further, almost every pupil at the fifth-grade level in social studies had some exposure to procedures for obtaining new information and the rudiments of reference skills. The extraordinarily heavy emphasis on algorithms and skills in math is also noteworthy.

Teacher Role and Simultaneous Segments

Until now we have been looking at segment properties primarily from the point of view of the students. How is the teacher's role coordinated with these arrangements? We slightly modified Gump's (1967) categories for teacher leadership patterns to answer this question (table 3.4).

As would be expected from what we already know, in the majority of segments in both subjects, teachers either played a watcher-helper role or were recitation leaders. However, social studies teachers were somewhat less active than math teachers, as evidenced by the larger percentage of segments in which they served as action directors and watcher-helpers (59 versus 38 percent for the categories combined). The social studies teachers coordinated and orchestrated classroom activities more than math teachers did. Another difference worth noting is that math teachers were absent from 14 percent of segments, while social studies teachers absented themselves from only 4 percent. Overall, the math teachers seemed to do slightly more teaching in front of the class and to be more active when working with a group than social studies teachers. But math teachers also left students on their own more.

Another way to look at the teacher's time and dispersion of energy is to examine the occurrence of simultaneous segments in the classroom. Whole-class segments accounted for slightly more than half the segments in both subjects (51 percent in math, 58 percent in social studies). In terms of student occupancy time, children in math classes were in whole-class segments 63 percent of the time; the comparable figure for social studies was 81 percent. The whole-class segments tended to be longer (table C.2) and to account for more student time in social studies. Also, there were often multiple simultaneous segments in social studies, while in math the typical pattern was a two-segment activity structure.

The structure of a math class with simultaneous segments is relatively simple from the teacher's point of view. In math, 24 percent of the segments occurred within a two-segment activity pattern, and an additional 16 percent in a three-segment activity pattern. Instances of more than three simultaneous segments were rare. In a typical two-segment pattern, the teacher worked with one group of children while the remainder of the class did a seatwork assignment. Another common two-segment pattern found the teacher working with the majority of the class while a few children worked on their own in a math laboratory or did advanced work. In a three-segment math pattern, the teacher typically worked with one group while two other groups worked independently. Although individualized programs in which each child worked at his own rate could be considered multiple simultaneous segments, each with one child as a member, we have not treated them as such. From the teacher's point of view, the instructional and management demands of individualized seatwork may be somewhat greater than a whole-class uniform seatwork segment, but they are surely not comparable to those entailed in running twenty-five simultaneous segments.

In social studies classes, when more than one segment was in progress, there were likely to be several. In the two-segment pattern typically found in math, the teacher belonged in one segment and had peripheral connections to the other. In social studies, the situation was quite different. A number of groups (often as many as six, seven, or eight) worked simultaneously, and the teacher had to monitor and assist them all. Typically the teacher either rotated from group to group or stayed in one spot, expecting children to come with questions and requests. Creating an effective activity structure with multiple simultaneous segments requires adequate preparation of the students. We often saw task preparation segments for the whole class preceding the launch of multiple segments. Since the teacher was less available to each group as it began operation, the quality of task preparation segments was crucial for promoting effective work.

SEGMENT PATTERNS

The coded segment features have been described singly, but the reader is reminded that all the variables were coded on the same set of segments and are not independent. Each feature adds some information to the description of instructional settings, but a useful next step is an examination of segment patterns. How do the activity segment features occur together?

Segment arrays were formed by creating all combinations of pacing, format, teacher leadership pattern, student behavior pattern, cognitive level, and expected student interaction. The number of segments, the percentage of segments, and the percentage of occupancy time were calculated for each pattern that resulted from combining the six variables. Table 3.5 lists segment patterns that accounted for either more than 2.5 percent of the segments in each subject or more than 2.5 percent of student occupancy time. For the purposes of this discussion, such segments have been designated as having high frequency patterns.[6]

If all combinations of categories of the six variables occurred, 396,032 possible patterns of segments would be present. In fact a very small number of patterns were found in both subjects, and this was especially true in math. Thirteen patterns met the "high frequency" criteria, accounting for about two-thirds of student occupancy time in math and 50 percent of all math segments. The earlier impression of repetitiveness in the child's math class experiences is reinforced by these findings on segment patterns.

Child-paced uniform seatwork segments, with students at their desks solving problems to develop mastery of concepts and skills, is the most common math segment pattern, accounting for one-fourth of student math time. The teacher was present in some segments as an occasional helper and supervisor and absent in others. In a small percentage of these seatwork segments, children were allowed limited interaction with one another for work-related purposes, but in most segments no interaction between pupils was permitted.

Individualized seatwork segments accounted for another frequent pattern (approximately 12 percent occupancy time) in math classes. As with uniform seatwork segments, students worked on concepts and skills as cognitive goals, and student interaction was very infrequent. Whereas the teacher was sometimes occupied in other settings when children were in uniform seatwork segments, pupils in individualized seatwork segments almost always had the teacher available in the watcher-helper role. Teachers rarely absented themselves from individualized seatwork settings to work with individuals or lead recitations.

Almost a fourth of student occupancy time in math classes went to teacher-paced recitations aimed at mastery of concepts and skills. Students did not interact with one another. They answered and asked questions, solved problems at their desks and at the blackboard, and watched problems being solved at the blackboard.

Two other patterns occurred often enough in math classes to appear on the high frequency list. During about 3 percent of student's time, they took tests; teacher-led checking of work segments accounted for another 3 percent of student time.

Ten patterns of segments in social studies occurred often enough

Table 3.5. High Frequency Segment Patterns

Pacing	Format	Teacher Role	Student Behavior	Cognitive Level	Student Interaction	N	Segments (%)	Occupancy Time (%)
			Mathematics					
Teacher	Recitation	Recit. Leader	Quest./Ans.	Concepts	None	45	8.43	7.57
Teacher	Recitation	Recit. Leader	Solve/Desk	Concepts	None	14	2.62	4.09
Teacher	Recitation	Recit. Leader	Blackboard/Solve	Concepts	None	19	3.56	4.74
Teacher	Recitation	Recit. Leader	Blackboard/Watch	Concepts	None	37	6.93	6.49
Teacher	Checking Work	Reader	Checking Work	Facts	None	19	3.56	2.57
Child	Seatwork	Not in	Solve/Desk	Concepts	None	39	7.30	5.62
Child	Seatwork	Watch/Help—Int.	Solve/Desk	Concepts	None	64	11.99	16.49
Child	Seatwork	Watch/Help—Int.	Solve/Desk	Concepts	Low	11	2.06	2.69
Child	Ind. Seatwork	Watch/Help—Int.	Solve/Desk	Concepts	None	31	5.81	5.28
Child	Ind. Seatwork	Watch/Help—Int.	Solve/Desk	Concepts	Low	5	0.94	2.62
Child	Ind. Seatwork	Watch/Help—Cont.	Solve/Desk	Concepts	None	8	1.50	3.80
Child	Test	Tester	Test	Concepts	None	9	1.69	3.14
Cooperative	Contest	Watch/Help—Int.	Game—Cog.	Concepts	Med.	15	2.81	0.99
Total						316	59.20	66.09

Social Studies

Teacher	Recitation	Recit Leader	Quest./Ans.	Facts	None	17	3.12	2.93
Teacher	Recitation	Recit Leader	Quest./Ans.	Concepts	None	13	2.39	3.48
Teacher	Recitation	Recit Leader	Read/Oral	Concepts	None	5	0.92	3.32
Teacher	Recitation	Recit Leader	Q/A—Oral Reading	Facts	None	16	2.94	4.83
Teacher	Recitation	Recit Leader	Q/A—Oral Reading	Concepts	None	11	2.02	4.55
Teacher	Giving Instr.	Action Director	Listening	Facts	None	21	3.85	1.56
Child	Seatwork	Watch/Help—Int.	Maps	Symbolic	None	9	1.65	4.48
Cooperative	Group Work	Watch/Help—Int.	Draw/Paint	Not Cog.	Med.	17	3.12	1.86
Cooperative	Group Work	Watch/Help—Int.	Game—Cog.	Application	Med.	19	3.49	0.50
Mechanical	Film/AV	Action Director	Film/AV	Facts	None	14	2.57	3.94
Total						142	26.07	31.45

Note: High frequency patterns are those that account for either more than 2.5 percent of the segments or more than 2.5 percent of student occupancy time. Terms are defined in appendix B.

to meet the high frequency criteria; together, they accounted for slightly less than one-third of the student occupancy time and 26 percent of all social studies segments. Many more combinations of segment feature properties occurred in social studies, and fewer patterns predominated. Table 3.5 shows that no one pattern accounts for as much as 5 percent of student time in the subject.

Some variety of teacher-led recitation was the pattern occurring most frequently in social studies lessons. During recitations, students might be involved in answering questions, reading orally, or some combination of the two. Relatively more frequent were recitations involving factual responses or at the comprehension level.

The only prevalent child-paced pattern in social studies was one that involved students in symbolic activity with maps. The high frequency cooperative segments had both application aims and not-cognitive goals, and involved games and art activities. Watching films also occurred enough to qualify as a high frequency pattern. It should be noted again, however, that no social studies pattern occurred very often overall, though in individual classrooms certain patterns were recurrent.

We found 110 different combinations of the six features in math; in social studies 140 segment types were identified. Gump (1967) also found relatively few patterns of action in the third-grade classrooms he studied. In our segments, pattern changes were at times relatively minor, but the social studies settings were clearly more diverse. Students and teachers experienced more types of action patterns in social studies classes than in math classes, and their actions were spread more evenly across segment varieties. Given the extremely large number of possible patterns, instruction in both subjects is mightily constrained, but the limits are particularly evident in the math classrooms.

PROGRAM VARIANTS

Another way to consider the question of segment patterns is to identify program variants or distinctive curricular approaches in each field of study. Major program variants in instructional approach were present in both math and social studies. In math, two program variants were identified. A traditional or teacher-directed whole-class approach was the most common. [7] Fifteen of the twenty classes conformed to the traditional pattern, with students spending at least 60 percent occupancy time in a combination of recitation, seatwork, checking work, or tests. The activities in these settings were highly repetitive. Teachers typically presented new concepts or material and reviewed through the use of a recitation, and then pupils worked individually on a written problem set at their desks. In some classes, the period began with checking homework, a time during which the teacher might provide some conceptual or procedural review. Students usually worked on the same assignments in these classes, and they were typically organized around the use of a textbook and/or workbook. However, in a few cases individuals or subgroups were given different assignments, usually for remediation or enrichment.

The other math program variant, individualized instruction, was used exclusively in four classes and for a significant amount of student time in a fifth class. (The four completely individualized classes, taught by teachers K., L., and M., are marked on figure 3.1.) Two teacher-centered classes had a small proportion of time in which students did individualized work also.

Individualized math programs consist of materials intended to enable students to master a sequence of instructional goals at their own rate. Students take pretests and posttests regularly. Their performance indicates whether they will work on the objective tested or move on to the next one in the sequence. The tests are used along with materials that provide practice for the students. In the cases we observed, all pupils traversed the same sequence of instructional steps. The materials varied in quality and composition in the individualized classes. In one class a standard commercial package was used, another had a district-made set of books and other materials, while a third drew from a large assortment of texts and resources collected by the teacher over a number of years.

The individualized programs were arranged to accommodate differences in rates of learning and to some extent to meet pupils' needs for different learning materials. Children in individualized math classes spent most of their time working on their own in individualized seatwork segments. Observers often felt they had entered a setting that resembled a factory with students laboring on a piecework contract, despite the richness of the materials available in some cases. Social interaction played no part in these individualized classes; the programs were designed to be full instructional systems. The teacher was not expected to provide developmental or introductory lessons like those seen in whole-class math instruction.

The teachers we observed behaved somewhat differently from each other in the individualized settings. In one case, the teacher stayed at her desk and was available to pupils who had questions or needed assistance. This teacher basically served as a supervisor and provided help when students requested it. Otherwise, she kept track of the students' performance as they moved through an elaborate cafeteria of materials she had thoughtfully accumulated. In another case, the teacher circulated among pupils and would create small groups of children for instruction at the blackboard as she felt it was needed. Another teacher directed pupils to audio tapes containing explanations of concepts or operations; the tapes served as substitutes for teacher presentations of content.

The two program variants in math—teacher-centered and individualized instruction—shared a common set of topics and objectives. As can be seen by reviewing the contents of figure 3.1, students in both variants worked on the same math skills and topics, notably operations with fractions and decimals. Adopting an individualized math program generally meant giving more attention to discrepancies in pupils' rates of learning, but goals for students were quite uniform across program variants.

As we observed them, individualized programs were somewhat more expensive and relied on technology, including advanced materials design, audiovisual equipment, and, in the latest versions, personal computers. However, new topics—such as more problem solving, geometry, analysis of data, or measurement—were not added to the individualized math programs as a result.

The two types of math instruction are likely to convey different messages to pupils about how one learns math. In the traditional case, an almost exclusive reliance on the teacher for introduction to new topics and procedures is communicated. In the individualized programs, math concepts are conveyed by materials. In both, however, children are restricted in their routes to learning math, a liability discussed in detail in our final chapter.

The social studies classes could be divided by predominant formats into three program variants: traditional, group work, and mixed format classes. The classes in each program variant are identified in figure 3.2. Across the nineteen classes, ten conformed to the traditional (teacher-centered) pattern, six had children working in face-to-face groups frequently (group-work pattern), and three classes showed a mixture of many formats (mixed format pattern). The ten teacher-centered classes in social studies were similar in format to those in mathematics. Whole-class instruction consisting of recitations and seatwork were the ingredients of the typical day. At least 60 percent of student time was spent in recitations and seatwork in these traditional classes. History and geography were common, although not exclusive, topics in the teacher-centered classes. (For topics, see classes marked traditional in figure 3.2.) Although similar to math recitations, those in social studies classes more often involved the use of the textbook. Children read in turn from textbooks and orally answered questions from the textbook or teacher.

The six group-work classes sometimes used curricular programs that had been written with group problem solving in mind. (For topics, see classes designated as group work in figure 3.2.) *Man: A Course of Study (MACOS)* and the curriculum based on a simulation of settling in the New World seen in Mrs. K.'s class both assumed that children would work together. A class engaged in exploring careers was organized in pairs or triplets for that purpose, while another class making crafts materials had some children collaborating and others working alone. Neither the career projects nor the craft projects required joint work as similar topics appeared in whole-class settings; teachers made the instructional choice.

There does seem to be a tendency for topics dealing with culture and society, civics, and psychology to appear in group-work or mixed format classes. The group-work curricula, such as *MACOS*, are also distinctive in their strong emphasis on group problem solving and higher mental process objectives. As we shall see in more detail in the next chapter, peer work groups have a high proportion of more complex intellectual goals (see also Graybeal and Stodolsky 1985).

The three mixed format social studies classes could not easily be labeled traditional or group work. These classes had some features of both. In math, some traditional classes had an occasional individualized segment, but the three mixed social studies classes seemed more generally eclectic than those math cases. The mixed format social studies classes also seemed topically distinct from teacher-centered classes.

Program variants in social studies did not lead to wholly unique experiences in the subject. Of note is that research skills were a component of almost every social studies program, whether a class was traditional or used peer work groups. Students used such reference materials as encyclopedias, dictionaries and atlases to obtain information for research papers or reports. Most students were expected to learn how to obtain information from a variety of sources and to interpret data and read maps and charts. In seatwork settings, even when children worked on their own, they were likely to make use of more resources in social studies than in an analogous math setting.

INDIVIDUAL TEACHERS

There is no doubt that math and social studies activity structures look different when we compare average classrooms. But the differences evident at the group level could result if only a few teachers radically altered their methods from one subject to the other. Did most teachers change the organization of instruction as they switched from math to social studies, or did only a few teachers skew the picture?

Fifteen teachers identified as A through O in figure 3.5 taught both subjects. Most of them created activity structures with features distinct to each field. This finding is illustrated by data on such key variables as pacing, cognitive level, instructional format, student behavior, and use of materials.

The distribution of pacing in the math and social studies classes of each teacher is a general assessment of the mode of teaching across the two fields. The ratio of teacher to child pacing in the two subjects is a useful index of the similarity of pacing. Figure 3.5 is a scatter plot of the ratios (natural log transformed) of teacher to child pacing in math and social studies. If teachers had similar pacing arrangements in the two subjects, the plot would be a line through the origin. Decided nonlinearity shows that the pacing conditions in the two areas are different for almost every one of the fifteen teachers.

To round out the picture of individual teachers' pacing decisions, cooperative and mechanical (audiovisual) pacing must also be surveyed. Both are used preferentially and often exclusively in social studies. Ten of the fifteen teachers used cooperative pacing. Five of the ten had cooperative segments only in social studies (C, G, L, M, O); the other five (A, E, F, J, K) used them in both subjects but in greater proportion in social studies. Six instructors (B, F, I, L, M,

Figure 3.5. Ratio of Teacher/Child Pacing in Two Subjects for Individual Teachers

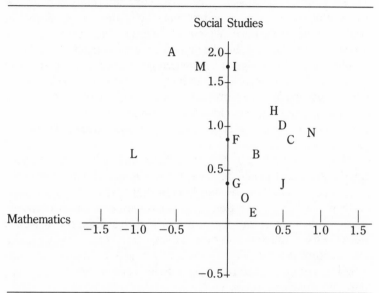

Social Studies

Mathematics

Note: Ratios are natural log-transformed. Each point represents one teacher's ratio in mathematics and social studies. Teacher K's ratio was zero and could not be plotted.

N) incorporated mechanical pacing into their programs, but this happened only in social studies.

Five teachers (B, C, D, J, N) looked very much alike in format use in the two subjects, while ten showed distinctive format distributions in each subject. Four of the five teachers who showed conformity across subjects relied on recitation and seatwork in both subjects. Within this traditional approach, however, there was a lack of similarity in cognitive goals, variability of materials, and diversity in expected student behaviors in the same teacher's classes.

A strong contrast can be drawn between traditional or teacher-centered instruction and classes organized around group work. One of our teachers (F) taught math in a highly traditional manner and used group work for social studies instruction. Two other teachers (K, L) had individualized math programs and group-work social studies programs. These two teachers, and two others (A, M) whose classes provided a similar contrast of smaller magnitude, are individuals whose teaching practices are "modern" for each field. These teachers' classes are structured very differently in math and social studies, but the teachers may be acting on a consistent nontraditional preference. We could discern no obvious pedagogical predilection in the instructional behaviors of the remaining teachers.

We already know that the cognitive goals of math segments can almost all be categorized as learning concepts and skills. Social studies lessons involve a greater number of intellectual processes. An examination of the cognitive levels of segments in each teacher's classes confirms that every teacher differs in the goals addressed in the two fields.

The data in table 3.3 on student behaviors in individual classes clearly show that pupils did different things in the math and social studies classes of the same teacher. In almost all cases they solved problems in math, but a wide variety of other behaviors occurred in social studies. Similarly, figure 3.3 shows that different materials were used by students under the tutelage of the same teacher in the two content areas. Many teachers did use textbooks in both subjects, but other materials appeared in social studies classes that were not present in math.

The children we studied really had different experiences in math and social studies lessons with the same teacher. For some, the contrast was dramatic. For almost all, the activity structures were different in important and noticeable ways. At a minimum the pacing distribution, student behavior, and cognitive goals varied from subject to subject.

Although student involvement will be analyzed thoroughly in the next chapter, another way to examine consistency in individual teachers is to use our involvement data. The students' involvement in the math and social studies classes of each of the teachers has been analyzed (Stodolsky 1984b). It is often assumed that teachers will be either generally good or generally poor at holding students' attention and keeping them involved in classroom activity. A high positive correlation between student involvement in the math and social studies classes taught them by the same teacher would favor the premise that even when teaching different subjects, teachers have a consistent immediate effect on students.

For the fifteen teachers who taught both subjects, the correlation between the average involvement in the two weeks of classes observed in math and the two weeks of classes in social studies was

.09, indistinguishable from zero. Teachers are not simply unstable in their teaching: the correlation between student involvement in the first week of classes and the second week of classes in math is .60, p < .01, and the correlation between involvement in the first and second weeks of social studies classes is .61, p < .01. These surprising results support the contention that there is a substantial change in practice by individual teachers as they change subjects of instruction, and pupils respond to each setting independently.

Most of the teachers altered their behavior and classroom arrangements by subject matter. A global variable like pacing produces data that are totally consistent with the claim, as does cognitive level. The distributions of instructional format used by each of the teachers who taught both subjects show that for two-thirds (ten) of the teachers, format use differed by subject. One-third (five) tended to use similar formats in the two subjects, although time allocated to the formats differed. Student behaviors were distinct in all fifteen classes. In social studies materials were more varied or different than those found in math classes. Beyond features of the classrooms, children's involvement in the two subjects taught by the same teacher was uncorrelated. Thus, data at the aggregate level and on individual teachers show a comprehensive effect of subject matter on how instruction takes place.

SUMMARY

The daily experiences of students and teachers were different in math and social studies. Instructional arrangements varied when different subjects were taught in elementary school. Almost every feature of the activity segments we observed was distinct in math classes and social studies classes, even though in most instances the same teachers taught both subjects.

Overall, we found more variety in social studies instruction than in math instruction. Diversity was apparent across social studies classes as well as within them. In many respects, math classes were more similar to one another. However, in both subjects, an extremely small number of instructional patterns were used given the possible alternatives available.

Program variants, based on the predominant formats used in classes, were identified in both subjects. In math, two program variants, traditional (teacher-centered) and individualized instruction, were in use. Most math classes (fifteen) were teacher-centered, favoring whole-class instruction with seatwork and recitations. In social studies, we found three program variants: traditional (teacher-centered), group-work, and mixed format classes. Ten of the nineteen social studies classes were teacher-centered, with heavy use of textbooks, recitations, and other teacher-directed activities. Six classes used group work, with much student time in small, face-to-face groups. Three classes were mixed format and combined many different instructional activities.

A finding worthy of note is that the relationship between content or topical coverage and program variants was not the same in math and social studies. In math, topics, sequences of instruction, and intellectual goals conformed across classrooms regardless of program variant. Though the majority of math teachers followed a traditional approach, individualized math programs embraced the same content and objectives found in traditional classes. Program variants were not related to content as such—content was quite uniform across all math classes.

In social studies, a distinctive teaching approach was accompanied by more differences in topics, cognitive goals, and materials than in math. The program variants in social studies often had dissimilar content with distinct disciplinary origins. History and geography tended to be taught in traditional classes. Group-work classes drew on psychology, anthropology, and more interdisciplinary perspectives for their content. But there were some important exceptions. Current events, and certain aspects of history, geography, and economics, were covered in both kinds of classes. Also, some group work had very limited intellectual content or dealt with special topics such as the study of careers.

The teachers we saw, teaching the same children in the same physical settings, typically used different classroom arrangements in math and social studies. When individual teachers shifted from one content area to the other, they varied cognitive goals, instructional formats, student behaviors, materials, and the extent to which pupils worked together. We have shown beyond a doubt that individual teachers do not use a consistent instructional approach all day long. What they are teaching shapes the way they teach.

The analysis of individual teachers' classes also revealed that students are not consistently involved or uninvolved in a given teacher's classroom. A surprising result was that the average involvement levels of students in a teacher's math class and the same teacher's social studies class were completely uncorrelated.

4

Beyond Subject Matter:
Intellectual Activity
and Student Response

The reader is now familiar with the pattern of subject matter differences in instructional segment features. Two very important issues that go beyond subject matter differences have been reserved for this chapter. The arrangement of the educational environment to attain different intellectual goals is the focus of the first part of the chapter. This part includes an analysis of the joint distribution of pacing and cognitive level, so that we can discover whether different intellectual goals are sought when teachers direct segments, when students work on their own, and when students work cooperatively. The relationship between instructional format and intellectual goals will also be examined.

We turn to student response to instructional arrangements in the second part of the chapter. Did students respond to the variation we have found across subject matters and to differing segment features within subjects, or did they sit out their days in school without consistently altering their reactions to the passing events? In line with the argument presented in chapter 1, we will specifically examine student involvement in relation to the cognitive level or complexity of segments, in relation to who is pacing the segments, and in relation to the need for the information contained in segments.

Looking at student involvement in relation to the setting permits us to see whether different educational arrangements produce differences in one type of behavioral response. One goal of educators is to engage students in educational pursuits, and altering educational procedures is often seen as a mechanism for enhancing student involvement. Our analyses will contribute to understanding the connections between student involvement and manipulable features of educational settings.[1]

HOW LEARNING ENVIRONMENTS
ARE ORGANIZED

Swings of opinion about how education should take place and what should be taught are a regular occurrence, well documented by historians of education (Church and Sedlak 1976). The depth of actual changes in school activities in different opinion climates has been creatively investigated by Cuban (1984). He concluded that student-centered practices were introduced in a limited number of classrooms and districts during the last century, but that the persistent daily problems of teachers faced with two to four dozen children often led to somewhat peripheral, rather than central, changes in educational practice. Where change seemed profound, teachers made a personal commitment to a new way of working with children, or they worked in an institutional setting that supported student-centered education and teachers and administrators helped one another achieve that end. In most schools, teacher-centered practices have persisted.

At times the research community has had a substantial impact on public stances toward education. The precise role the researcher should play in policy discourse will not be debated here,[2] but we can agree that interpretations of research data should enter into policy making. Descriptive evidence about how instruction takes place in schools is particularly important in a policy context that requires knowledge about the tendencies of practitioners to adopt alternative ways of working. Knowledge of how educators work or have worked over periods of time can suggest factors that have influenced instructional settings and the behavior of their participants.

A recent and influential example of a research-derived prescription for educational practice is the direct instruction model, an empirically based amalgam of suggestions for effective instruction. The direct instruction model includes a set of instructional variables found to positively correlate with gains in student achievement on standardized tests of elementary mathematics and reading (Rosenshine 1976; Berliner 1979). To formulate the direct instruction model, Rosenshine incorporated findings from the Follow Through evaluation (Stallings and Kaskowitz 1974), the Beginning Teacher Evaluation Study of second and fifth grades (Fisher et al. 1978), and research by Soar and Soar (1976), among others.

Rosenshine (1979) describes the recommended classroom procedures:

Direct instruction refers to academically focused, teacher-directed classrooms using sequenced and structured materials. It refers to teaching activities where goals are clear to students, time allocated for instruction is sufficient and continuous, coverage of content is extensive, the performance of students is monitored, questions are at a low cognitive level so that students can produce many correct responses and feedback to students is immediate and academically oriented. In direct instruction the teacher controls instructional goals, chooses materials appropriate for the student's ability, and paces the instructional episode. Interaction is characterized as structured, but not authoritarian. Learning takes place in a convivial academic atmosphere. The goal is to move students through a sequenced set of materials or tasks. Such materials are common across classrooms and have a relatively strong congruence with the tasks on achievement tests (p. 38).

The intellectual level of instruction and the control of pacing are obviously central concerns in defining the direct instruction view of effective classroom arrangements. Teacher pacing, questions at a low cognitive level, and teacher specification of tasks, sequences, and structure are all ingredients of the model. The proponents of direct instruction assert that the arrangements described are most effective in producing achievement gains, particularly in math and reading.

The findings of Gump (1967) and Grannis (1978) provide some insight into why the particular components of the direct instruction model emerge in process-product studies of reading and math instruction in the early grades. Their behavior setting data showed that teacher pacing and low-level intellectual activities occurred together and dominated primary grade settings devoted to teaching math and reading. They also found that student involvement was highest when young students were under direct teacher supervision. Since Rosenshine summarized studies conducted primarily in traditional primary classrooms, it is not surprising that higher correlations with achievement were found for the conditions that are most frequently used in those classrooms and that are known to relate to student involvement within them. However, with other setting conditions, the correlations could look quite different—a point often overlooked by the consumers of correlational research.

Many observers bemoan the impoverished intellectual quality of schooling, particularly at the elementary level. They point to an overemphasis on factual knowledge, neglect or even destruction of creativity, and a lack of real inquiry or complexity in the curriculum (e.g., Goodlad 1984). Regarding intellectual activity in the large number of schools he studied, Goodlad (1984, p. 236) comments:

> Only *rarely* did we find evidence to suggest instruction likely to go much beyond mere possession of information to a level of understanding its implications and either applying it or exploring its possible applications. Nor did we see activities likely to arouse students' curiosity or to involve them in seeking solutions to some problem not already laid bare by teacher or textbook.
>
> And it appears that this preoccupation with the lower intellectual processes pervades social studies and science as well. An analysis of topics studied and materials used gives not an impression of students studying human adaptations and explorations but of facts to be learned.

As we have seen, the very qualities of schooling that Goodlad is concerned about have significant support in educational circles and in the public arena. The direct instruction model incorporates many of the features seen as problematic by Goodlad and other educators. There is no consensual vision of ideal schooling in our society.

More empirical data will not in themselves alter educational philosophies, but information about classroom practice can sharpen questions and at times redirect thinking about problems. Our data permit a detailed look at the relations between pacing conditions, cognitive goals, and subject matter. This more focused analysis of classroom instruction may be helpful to those considering educational alternatives. We also need to compare our results with those of other researchers to see whether the low level of intellectual activity typical in other situations is present in our classes.

Cognitive Level and Pacing

The distributions of pacing and cognitive level were described in the last chapter (see table 3.4). Every cognitive level was present in the pool of social studies segments: segments with no cognitive goal, those emphasizing facts, those oriented to comprehension or concepts, those in which students learned research skills, and those containing application or other higher mental process activities were all found. In contrast, the cognitive goals of math segments were restricted. Most math segments involved learning concepts and skills, some were at the factual level, and a very small number entailed application of concepts and skills. No other cognitive level was addressed in the math classes.

The distribution of pacing was likewise distinct in the two subject fields. Teacher, child, cooperative, and mechanical pacing each occurred in some social studies segments. Mechanical pacing did not occur in math, and cooperative pacing was very infrequent and restricted to game activities. Not unexpectedly, teacher and child pacing were common in the math classrooms.

Were the conditions under which pupils work toward different cognitive levels similar, or did the arrangement of activity segments vary with the objective of the activity? Did teachers believe certain curricular objectives to be best achieved by having children work on their own or cooperatively, while others are better taught by direct teacher presentation or recitation? Were arrangements made for a given cognitive objective the same in math as in social studies?

The distribution of cognitive levels of tasks in each of the pacing conditions[3] is displayed by subject matter in table 4.1. Since social studies shows the most variety in cognitive level, we examine it first.

A highly regular pattern emerges in the social studies data. Teacher-paced segments occurred primarily at the lower cognitive levels, with more than half consisting of receiving or recalling information. While the teacher was directing segments (e.g., recitations, giving instructions, task preparations), children were mostly expected to master factual information. Some teacher-led segments involved learning concepts, while a smaller number dealt with symbolic and graphic research skills and higher mental processes.

The child-paced segments were more evenly distributed across cognitive levels. Children working on their own engaged in activities at all cognitive levels. They were most frequently found conducting research activities, receiving information, and learning concepts and skills. Activities with the most complex goals (application and other higher mental processes) occurred less often, as did not-cognitive segments.

Table 4.1. Distribution and Mean Involvement of Cognitive Levels by Pacing

	Pacing														
	Teacher					Child					Cooperative				
Cognitive Level[a]	N	% Col.	% Row	$\overline{X}$ Inv.[b]	S.D. Inv.	N	% Col.	% Row	$\overline{X}$ Inv.[b]	S.D. Inv.	N	% Col.	% Row	$\overline{X}$ Inv.[b]	S.D. Inv.
Social Studies:	(% Occupancy Time = 47.5)					(% Occupancy Time = 33.5)					(% Occupancy Time = 12.5)				
Not Cognitive	—	—	—	—	—	8	7.5	17.4	53.9	27.3	38	19.9	82.6	73.7	22.9
Receive/Recall Facts	131	58.2	82.4	75.3	21.3	24	22.6	15.1	68.9	21.9	4	2.1	2.5	66.7	36.3
Learn Concepts/ Skills	40	17.8	43.5	73.5	17.1	24	22.6	26.1	76.2	22.0	28	14.7	30.4	82.4	14.6
Research Skills	28	12.4	32.2	74.6	19.9	39	36.8	44.8	78.0	14.1	20	10.5	30.0	84.3	15.1
Application and Higher Mental Processes	26	11.6	18.8	76.0	23.8	11	10.3	8.0	74.9	13.5	101	52.9	73.2	83.7	22.1
Mathematics:	(% Occupancy Time = 44.7)					(% Occupancy Time = 51.2)					(% Occupancy Time = 4.1)				
Receive/Recall Facts	86	32.6	95.5	67.5	23.3	4	1.8	4.5	93.8	5.6	—	—	—	—	—
Learn Concepts/ Skills	169	64.0	39.5	77.3	15.8	216	96.0	50.5	79.4	13.9	43	95.6	10.0	83.8	22.7
Application and Higher Mental Processes	9	3.4	56.3	85.3	10.6	5	2.2	31.2	73.3	11.5	2	4.4	12.5	85.6	1.5

[a]Levels are defined in appendix B.
[b]Mean involvement is calculated for fewer than N segments because of missing observations.

The cooperatively paced segments in social studies show a very different distribution of cognitive levels. Children working with one another were given complex tasks, the majority of them with application and higher mental processes as objectives. However, 20 percent of the segments in which children engaged jointly were coded not cognitive. The cooperative condition thus tended toward the bimodal, encompassing the two extremes of cognitive level more than the other pacing conditions. But most activities of children working in groups were cognitively complex, dramatically more so than in either of the other pacing conditions, but especially more than in the teacher-paced segments.

The row percentages in table 4.1 highlight the systematic variation of cognitive level with pacing. Over 80 percent of the segments in which students learned facts or obtained basic information were teacher-directed. The activity of learning concepts and skills was fairly evenly divided among the three pacing conditions, although more of the segments were teacher-paced. Students were asked to work on their own somewhat more often when research skills were the goal, although this objective occurred in all three pacing categories. A major shift occurred when application and higher mental processes were sought. Almost three-quarters of these most cognitively complex segments were cooperatively paced. Over 80 percent of the segments with no discernible cognitive goal also occurred in the cooperative context.

In social studies, different settings were established to foster different objectives. It may be some cause for concern that the lowest cognitive objectives were addressed in the teacher-led segments. On the other hand, the most cognitively complex tasks were usually given to children to solve cooperatively, usually through small-group discussion.

In math, students' main activity centered on learning and practicing skills and algorithms (*Taxonomy* level two). Although the objectives in math were very restricted, was there any relation between pacing and cognitive level? A smaller proportion of segments were coded "factual" in math than in social studies. However, the teacher-paced condition accounted for almost all math segments (96 percent) for which receiving or recalling facts was the goal. About one-third the teacher-paced segments were at the factual level. Learning concepts and skills occurred in all three pacing conditions, but most of the segments were child- or teacher-paced. Application segments were very rare; only sixteen were identified.

They occurred in all pacing conditions but were more frequent in teacher pacing.

Both subjects showed a strong tendency for the teacher to direct the activity segments at the lowest cognitive level. In social studies, where many different cognitive goals occur, the teacher-directed segments were mostly at the lowest levels. Most math segments fell at *Taxonomy* level two, but almost every factual segment was led by the teacher. Cognitively complex tasks occurred only in social studies, where they were the strong province of cooperative work groups.

The pattern in the data suggests that students will expect to work differently as pacing changes. The type of task and the expected cognitive processes are the major differences. If complexity and challenge go hand in hand, children can expect the least challenge when under teacher direction in both subjects, variety and middle level challenge when working on their own in both subjects, and the highest levels of cognitive challenge when working with one another in social studies.

The educational arrangements established for the pursuit of different intellectual objectives are not haphazard. It is worth exploring why the distribution of pacing and cognitive goals is so asymmetric. Later in this chapter, the formats used in teacher-paced segments will be examined. Uncovering the pedagogical purposes of teacher-paced segments helps explain the pronounced patterned relationship between who paces activity and the intellectual level of the tasks pursued. Now, however, we turn to an analysis of student involvement.

STUDENT INVOLVEMENT

In this section we ask, How do children respond to segments with differing characteristics? How does student involvement vary with cognitive level, with pacing, and with combinations of these? Do students deploy their attention efficiently and with curiosity as we have suggested? Are students more attentive when faced with complex tasks? Are patterns of involvement similar in math and social studies? (Recall that we sampled students on a number of occasions during a segment to obtain our involvement data. Our involvement measure is thus the percent of observed occasions on which the observed students were on-task or otherwise engaged in acceptable behavior. When we present average involvement for a group of segments, such as a given cognitive level, we have averaged percentages calculated for each segment first. A higher involvement index thus likely reflects that more of the children observed were involved on more observation occasions than would be true with a lower index, and on average the group of segments is composed of individual segments in which students were found involved on more observation occasions.)

Although math and social studies are taught differently, the first finding of interest is that overall average involvement in the two subjects was very similar. Students paid the same amount of attention in our basic and enrichment subjects. The students we observed were engaged with the expected activities on more than three-quarters of the occasions we sampled their behavior.[4] Generally speaking, our students were involved in their school activities.

Cognitive Level, Pacing, and Student Involvement

We have hypothesized that children respond positively to cognitive complexity and challenge.[5] Average student involvement should increase with the steps of the cognitive hierarchy. The data showing our fifth graders' involvement are given in table 4.2.

In social studies, where there is the most diversity in cognitive level, there is a perfect correspondence between the rank order of complexity and the rank of student involvement. A more limited test is available in math, but the same pattern occurs. In both subjects an average of at least ten percentage points separates the highest and lowest cognitive levels. Since we have usually found subject matter differences, it is particularly striking that student response to cognitive level showed the same pattern in both subjects.

These data clearly indicate that children are more involved in activities with higher cognitive goals. The average level of attention seems graded to the level of complexity of the instructional activity. Cognitive complexity may be associated with higher involvement because the tasks are more difficult and require more attention and effort, and because children's interest is increased by more challenging or complicated tasks. Other features of the settings in which the tasks are accomplished may also play a significant role. Some clarification can be obtained by looking at the data further.

Since pacing is systematically related to cognitive level in our

Table 4.2. Mean Involvement by Complexity of Cognitive Levels

	Social Studies		
Cognitive Level[a]	N[b]	$\overline{X}$	S.D.
Not Cognitive	35	71.3	23.5
Receive/Recall Facts	178	74.9	21.2
Concepts/Skills	85	76.5	18.1
Research Skills	73	77.9	17.0
Application and Higher Mental Processes	118	81.3	22.1
Total	489	76.8	20.7
	Mathematics		
Receive/Recall Facts	84	68.4	23.4
Concepts/Skills	382	78.9	15.7
Application and Higher Mental Processes	16	81.6	11.3
Total	482	77.1	17.6

Note: A one-way ANOVA on cognitive level shows a significant effect on involvement in social studies ($F = 2.5$, $p < .05$) and in math ($F = 13.24$, $p < .0001$).
[a]Levels are defined in appendix B.
[b]N is the number of segments for which involvement estimates are available.

data, an examination of student involvement under different pacing conditions is the logical next step. Table 4.3 shows average student involvement as a function of type of pacing.

In the math segments, the teacher-paced segments have the lowest average involvement rates, the cooperative segments the highest. Student attention is also fairly high in the child-paced segments.[6]

Our data do not conform to patterns found by Gump (1967) and Fisher et al. (1978). Child-paced math segments, mostly seatwork, are more involving for our fifth graders than comparable settings studied with younger pupils. On the other hand, teacher-paced settings in our math classes do not produce the higher levels of student attention found in previous studies.

The difference in the grade levels studied is probably the best explanation for the discrepancies with other research. Fifth-grade children doing seatwork tasks usually expect that a certain amount of work must be accomplished per day or per week. If the work is not completed during school time, it becomes homework. In most primary classes, children work for a period of time, put the work away, and pick up where they left off during the next work period. Since fifth graders cannot avoid task accomplishment, they may work harder or more efficiently during time provided in school. Older children may also be better able to work independently. The fact that teacher pacing does not produce higher involvement in the math classes needs to be explained by a closer look at the particular types of segments run by math teachers.

Cooperative segments had the highest levels of involvement in both math and social studies.[7] Children apparently found small face-to-face work settings particularly engaging. In math, cooperative settings were infrequent, and usually games or contests. In social studies, group-work segments involving complex tasks and discussion were the norm.[8]

In addition to cooperative segments, social studies had three other pacing conditions (see table 4.3). Students showed high levels of attention in mechanical (audiovisual) settings. The difference between student involvement in child-paced and teacher-paced segments is very small.[9]

Teacher pacing produced about the same mean involvement (.75)

Table 4.3. Mean Involvement by Type of Pacing

Pacing[a]	Mathematics			Social Studies		
	N[b]	$\overline{X}$	S.D.	N[b]	$\overline{X}$	S.D.
Cooperative	34	83.9	22.0	149	81.7	20.7
Child	195	79.5	13.9	95	73.2	20.0
Teacher	253	74.4	19.0	222	75.0	20.7
Mechanical	—	—	—	23	79.7	17.1
Total	482	77.1	17.6	489	76.8	20.7

Note: A one-way ANOVA on pacing shows a significant effect in math ($F = 7.45$, $p < .001$) and in social studies ($F = 5.48$, $p < .001$).
[a]Terms are defined in appendix B.
[b]N is the number of segments for which involvement estimates are available.

in both math and social studies, whereas child-paced segments showed a higher average in math. Across fields, only cooperative pacing consistently related to higher levels of involvement, producing the highest average in both school subjects.

The joint distribution of cognitive level and pacing showed marked asymmetries. Cognitive levels were not equally represented in the pacing conditions. Can the difference in average involvement under different pacing arrangements be explained by the cognitive levels found in the segments? Alternatively, is there an independent contribution of pacing and cognitive level to student involvement? Table 4.1 displays the means for student involvement by subject matter, pacing, and each of the five cognitive levels used in the hierarchical analysis.

Cognitive level as such seems to play an important role in determining involvement in some of the pacing conditions but not in all. Both features, pacing and cognitive level, are important correlates of attention. In social studies, for example, teacher-paced segments produce moderate levels of attention in students irrespective of cognitive level. In math, however, the cognitive level of teacher-paced segments is clearly related to student involvement, with students exhibiting a pattern favoring complexity.

The need for information and the novelty of information were proposed earlier as features to which students respond. The function of the activities conducted by teachers may be a key to understanding the differing patterns of response in the two subjects. After looking at the other pacing conditions in relation to cognitive level, we will turn to a more detailed analysis of the teacher-led segments.

In both the child-paced and cooperatively paced social studies segments, children showed lower involvement when engaged in noncognitive or factual tasks and higher engagement with more complex tasks. Children working on their own or working together in groups had lower attention when assigned unchallenging, simpler tasks. Pacing and cognitive level both seem to contribute to student involvement in these segments. Students were more involved in cooperative settings as a whole, but their response was moderated by the complexity of the task. Similarly, child-paced tasks were somewhat less engaging in social studies, but the nature of the activity clearly affected their attention.

Since the other math segments show little variation in cognitive level, it is only possible to look at the teacher-paced segments from this point of view. Segments under teacher direction with low-level cognitive goals had much lower student involvement than those directed toward learning concepts and skills and application. We need more detail regarding exactly what activities teachers use at the factual level.

To summarize, student involvement related to both the cognitive level and the pacing of activity segments. More specifically, complexity and cooperation are keys to student responsiveness in math and social studies. A clear pattern of increasing student involvement as a function of cognitive complexity occurs in both subjects. There is also a consistent result with regard to pacing in both subjects. Children's average involvement was highest when they were working cooperatively.

An inconsistent pattern of involvement is present in the teacher-directed segments in the two subjects. Although children were involved to a similar degree in teacher-led activities in both subjects, cognitive level and complexity related to student involvement within teacher-paced math segments but not in teacher-paced social studies segments. In particular, math factual segments called forth a low level of attention, whereas no such reaction occurred in social studies. Two analyses may help to clarify these results. A closer look at the types of activities teachers pace at the factual level, to which we turn now, is the first analysis. An examination of cognitive level within recitation segments is presented afterward.

Factual Teacher-Paced Segments

Why were students less attentive to the low-level teacher-directed segments in math but not in social studies? What accounted for the discrepancy? What pedagogical functions were being served in teacher-led segments at the factual level?

We proposed that students behave efficiently in classrooms, adjusting their attention as needed to the flow of instruction and information. This leads us to ask, How do the factual segments fit in the flow of instruction, and how important or novel is the information they contain?

The formats used by teachers while directing factual segments were distributed differently in math and social studies (see table 4.4). Almost half the math segments dealt with checking work, and an additional third with giving instructions and task preparation. A small number of math recitations and lectures also fell at the factual level. In contrast, recitations occupied a third of the segments in

Table 4.4. Distribution of Formats in Teacher-Paced Segments at Factual Cognitive Level

	Social Studies						Mathematics					
Format[a]	N	Seg-ments (%)	$\bar{X}$ Duration	S.D. Duration	$\bar{X}$ Inv.[b]	S.D. Inv.	N	Seg-ments (%)	$\bar{X}$ Duration	S.D. Duration	$\bar{X}$ Inv.[b]	S.D. Inv.
Recitation	43	32.8	14.3	10.5	71.1	21.1	6	7.0	22.7	9.4	77.4	16.9
Giving Instructions	43	32.8	5.7	3.1	75.5	23.6	21	24.4	3.8	2.1	66.9	30.3
Task Preparation	13	9.9	7.9	2.9	82.8	15.4	9	10.5	4.7	2.5	57.3	30.5
Checking Work	11	8.4	10.7	5.7	82.5	5.3	40	46.5	9.7	5.6	66.1	18.1
Lecture	6	4.6	10.2	10.6	86.2	16.1	7	8.1	8.4	7.5	78.5	21.1
Student Reports	4	3.1	23.3	12.3	59.6	23.2	—	—	—	—	—	—
Discussion	3	2.3	8.3	5.0	56.4	36.6	—	—	—	—	—	—
Demonstration	3	2.3	20.0	11.8	56.3	—	1	1.2	6.0	—	100.0	—
Test	3	2.3	21.3	7.8	85.5	5.3	2	2.3	18.0	—	77.1	—
Film/Audiovisual	1	0.8	18.0	—	90.9	—	—	—	—	—	—	—
Seatwork	1	0.8	8.0	—	100.0	—	—	—	—	—	—	—
Total	131	100.0	10.8	8.8	75.3	21.3	86	100.0	8.7	7.0	67.5	23.3

[a]Terms are defined in appendix B.
[b]Mean involvement is calculated on slightly fewer than N segments due to missing observations.

social studies, and task preparation and giving instructions accounted for 43 percent of the segments. Checking work took up a relatively small percentage of the segments, and a smattering of other formats were also used.

The distribution of format categories in the factual-level segments provides a tentative explanation for the differences in student attention to these segments in math and social studies. Checking work, task preparation, and giving instructions accounted for a large proportion of the math segments and evoked low levels of attention in math. The same format categories represented a smaller percentage of social studies segments, but they had higher student attention there. Within and across the two subjects, student response to format categories varied, suggesting that an analysis of instructional function may be profitable. A scrutiny of the segments in format categories that produce discrepant responses in the two fields is a strategy for understanding the pattern better. Preparatory segments (giving instructions and task preparation) form a useful case, as do segments devoted to checking work.

Preparatory Segments

Preparatory segments were superficially similar in math and social studies, but their function in the flow of segments differed qualitatively. In math, preparatory segments usually occurred prior to seatwork and tended to be short (about four minutes). Typically students were told which problems to solve, when their work was due, and the form to follow. Occasionally the teacher briefly illustrated a solution or reminded students to be careful about a procedure. For example, a teacher might caution students to find the lowest common denominator in adding fractions. The preparatory segments were highly routinized and predictable. Students could readily ascertain or predict the information needed to do the succeeding seatwork or homework assignment. The textbook or worksheet often provided enough information for many students to proceed without teacher directions. The teacher characteristically communicated redundant, repetitive, and simple information.

In social studies many preparatory segments occurred prior to group-work activities, and they tended to be longer than those in math (about seven minutes). Group tasks and activities tended to be novel and complex; students really needed the information teachers provided in the preparatory segments in order to work together. For example, some segments dealt with details about how to play games, such as the Caribou Hunt that is part of the *MACOS* program, or provided directions for executing a project, such as making a booklet on black stars. Or recall Mrs. K.'s students being readied to make decisions about supplies for explorers' ships while involved in Sailing to the New World. These activities were not familiar and predictable, and the teacher's communications were more than reminders—they provided information that for nearly all pupils was both new and necessary. Since a broader range of activities occurred in social studies classes, at any time students were less likely to be in a predictable and routine activity, even in classes not using group work. Consequently, preparations were more likely to relate to newer tasks.

Although teacher messages to prepare students for subsequent activities were factual in both math and social studies, the information conveyed in the two areas differed in both novelty and necessity. Often, the information in social studies was essential; in math it was often predictable and redundant. The pedagogical function of the preparation segments in math was more perfunctory, seemingly reflexive.

Students' responses to preparatory segments followed their need for the information contained in them (see table 4.4). Lower rates of attention were associated with the math segments, while students were more attentive to preparation activities in social studies.[10] Within each context, apparently students responded to the functional demands of the segments in the instructional flow and not to their form alone. They were more attentive during task preparation when the information communicated was necessary or novel.

Checking-Work Segments

Checking work is the other main category of factual, teacher-led segments in math that produced low student involvement. The format "checking work" was coded when activity in a segment was restricted to correcting work; teachers did not explain why problems were correct or incorrect in these segments (such cases would have been coded recitations or lectures) but simply communicated answers or called on students to give answers. Ms. O.'s class provides a typical example of a check-work segment. Some such segments were reduced to exchanges about the mechanics of grading and whether someone could get credit under particular circumstances. Checking work in math is a routinized activity, with an action pattern that is not very demanding. It bores some students, particularly when it moves slowly, and such segments averaged ten minutes. The low student involvement in the math check-work segments indicates that students were adjusting their attention to the task demands here as they did in task preparation segments.

The small number of check-work segments in social studies had high student involvement. In several, students corrected tests or assignments that were somewhat unusual, such as crossword puzzles and rebus worksheets. Perhaps the materials were intrinsically more interesting or demanded more attention to the task, as when a student needed to decide if a particular definition should be considered correct. The less frequent occurrence of checking work may also have contributed to the higher level of student involvement.

The analysis of the check-work and preparatory segments must be considered exploratory in light of the relatively small numbers of segments in these categories. Nevertheless, the analysis suggests an explanation for both the cognitive-level effect in teacher-paced math segments and the difference in response to factual segments in math and social studies. The two types of activity that account for most of the factual math segments involve transmission of repetitive, redundant, or minimally necessary information to which students attend at low levels. When factual information is needed or novel, as occurs in social studies, students are more attentive. The general picture of higher involvement with higher cognitive level must be augmented by considering the functional and pedagogical importance of material. If factual information is important to the flow of the activity, students seem to adjust their attention upward. If factual information is redundant, repetitive, or parceled out slowly, students adjust their attention downward.

Recitation Segments

Recitations have long been of interest to instructional researchers (Hoetker and Ahlbrand 1969). About one-third of the teacher-paced social studies segments at the factual level are recitations. Within social studies, the factual recitations have below average student involvement. Recitations are thought to be an inherently (i.e., structurally) problematic educational format because it is difficult to involve students in an activity in which most of them are passive most of the time. Elsewhere we (Stodolsky, Ferguson, and

Wimpelberg 1981) have proposed that recitations nevertheless may serve important pedagogical functions.

Much of the criticism of recitations stems from the fact that the questions asked are usually at a low level. The poor quality and banality of the queries have led to some efforts at improving teachers' questioning skills (Gall 1970; Stano 1981). The recitations we observed can be examined to see what cognitive goals were addressed in the segments and whether student response varied within recitations as a function of their cognitive complexity.

The distribution of cognitive levels within recitations varied by subject matter, as it did in all instructional segments (see table 4.5). In math, most of the recitations aimed toward students' attainment of concepts and skills; a few were factual or involved application. In social studies, slightly under half the segments were factual, about one-third were at the comprehension level, and about a fourth were directed at more complex cognitive processes. Recitations were thus dominated by low-level questions in both subjects but were not purely factual. The majority involved comprehension or other cognitive skills in both subject matters.

Given the variation in levels of recitations, what did involvement look like as the cognitive level of the recitations went up? (See table 4.5.) In line with the thrust of this chapter, it was reasonable to expect that students would respond to the complexity of information content and process in recitation questions and tasks, not to the format alone.

Table 4.5. Mean Involvement in Recitations at Different Cognitive Levels

Cognitive Level[a]	Mathematics			Social Studies		
	N[b]	$\overline{X}$	S.D.	N[b]	$\overline{X}$	S.D.
Receive/Recall Facts	5	77.4	16.9	43	71.1	21.1
Concepts/Skills	135	76.8	15.6	30	72.1	16.3
Research Skills	—	—	—	10	80.5	21.3
Application and Higher Mental Processes	8	86.6	10.5	13	83.1	11.4

[a]Levels are defined in appendix B.
[b]N is the number of segments for which involvement estimates are available.

A very clear effect of cognitive level was evident in social studies recitations. Within a question-and answer format, the more complex the questions as judged by cognitive level, the higher the student involvement. More specifically, a substantially higher level of attention was paid to segments with research skills, application, and other higher mental processes as goals. Similarly in math, although the cognitive level range was more limited, the application segments had considerably higher mean involvement than those at the factual or conceptual levels.

Although teachers tend to ask factual and comprehension questions more frequently than application, analysis, or synthesis questions, higher-order questions clearly elicit higher levels of student attention. Within the same format, we saw students adjusting their attention to the demands of the task. As was true for all segments, greater cognitive complexity goes with higher student involvement, even within the oft-experienced recitation form.

Critics of recitations have focused on the fact that they consist of a passive activity pattern for students. The teacher is really the active person during a recitation. Any pupil may be waiting to be called on and attentive for that reason, but it takes a skilled recitation leader to have most students feel that it is "their" activity. However, our analysis shows that inherently more complex, and presumably more challenging, material will sustain student attention in the recitation, and low-level activity will lead to its diminution. Cognitive complexity is thus associated with greater student involvement in formats of all types, even the recitations that require a passive, listening behavior pattern most of the time.

DISCUSSION

A central goal of teachers is the establishment of educational conditions that engage students in meaningful learning activities. An understanding of how students respond to various classroom arrangements contributes to attaining this goal, along with a clear view of what is worth teaching and learning in the first place.

Prior research, reviewed in chapter 1, has tended to focus on involvement of young children in settings in which skill learning is emphasized. The data suggest that, in those restricted circumstances, students are most involved when under direct teacher supervision, when the teacher is active, and when they are pursuing tasks they can master with only moderate difficulty (Rosenshine

1979; Brophy and Good 1986). More limited data that tend to run counter to those results involve observations of students in nontraditional classrooms (Stallings and Kaskowitz 1974), students studying enrichment areas in which educational settings are frequently arranged differently than in basic skill subjects (Grannis 1978), and older students.

Our analysis of student involvement has tested the premise that students behave efficiently in deploying their attention and that they respond to complexity and its challenges. We also examined student involvement under different pacing conditions. With respect to information communicated in segments, students adjust their attention both to the complexity of the information and to the necessity for the information in the flow of a lesson. In addition, students find collaboration with one another engaging. Thus, our analysis creates a different picture of the circumstances that involve students than drawn by many prior investigators. The responsive student in our classrooms, however, lives up to the expectations of theorists who view students as efficient, curious, seeking challenge, and benefitting from cooperation and collaboration.

The Responsive Student

Students adjusted their energies and attention to features of setting activity. Perhaps our most striking finding is the completely consistent relationship between student involvement and cognitive complexity in both math and social studies. As cognitive complexity increased, so did children's average involvement. The pattern was also present within recitation segments themselves, particularly when one compared higher mental processes to lower ones. Similarly, group-work segments showed a sharp increase in student attention when higher mental processes were the goal.

The children we studied came from a relatively broad range of backgrounds and possessed diverse abilities. Were the findings confounded by underlying background differences in student involvement or school programs? Within and across socioeconomic levels, the relationship between cognitive complexity and student involvement was replicated; it was not an artifact of a relationship between home background and attention. Our sample showed no correlation between student involvement and the SES of the students. We did not find a regular relationship between curricular use and SES either.[11]

The students we observed were more engaged with complex and

challenging tasks than with simpler factual exercises. The analysis of student involvement in checking work and preparatory segments showed that students were efficient in their responses to information graded with respect to redundancy, novelty, and necessity. They were more engaged under conditions of novelty and complexity but paid less attention to information already known or easily obtained. The necessity of the information also affected the extent to which students monitored it closely.

Student involvement also differed depending on who was pacing the activity. In both social studies and math, cooperative activity was more involving than solitary or teacher-directed work, unless the collaborative tasks were essentially devoid of intellectual content.

It seems appropriate to suggest that teachers incorporate more challenging activities in their classrooms and make more use of cooperative arrangements. But teachers need to strike a balance in the day's activities. While students could undoubtedly profit from more complexity and challenging activity, the optimal balance of different activities is not immediately obvious and is not likely to be the same for all pupils. The reluctance of teachers to use group work must arise in part from a feeling of loss of control when youngsters are without direct supervision (cf. Cuban 1984). Although our data show that pupils generally were engaged in work-related activities in cooperative segments, the perceived potential for disruption is understandable if perhaps too pessimistic. Successful experience with group-work activities and mastery of management and instructional procedures to use with small groups would appear to be the best antidotes for the pessimism.

Aggregate student involvement levels paralleled those expected of an individual student. We do not really know whether the aggregate results indicate that some students did not pay any attention (for example, during preparation those who already knew how to do a math assignment) while others were very involved, or whether most students were less consistently attentive. A cursory examination of the data suggests that the latter explanation is more likely, but our method does not permit a definitive answer.

More research is needed to better understand the role of involvement or attention in the learning process. There is an implicit assumption in much educational research that more attention or higher levels of time on task should always be sought. [12] Those who assume that students should exhibit 100 percent on-task behavior (undivided attention) hold an overly simple view of processes integral to learning. Careful clinical studies of attention deployment are needed to understand how effective learners actually function. Indications in the literature and introspection suggest that learning and insight require both periods of active involvement and periods of withdrawal and reflection. More information about the deployment of attention during learning, obtained by more focused studies of individuals, would be profitable.

Although involvement has some universal connotations, its interpretation may have to be restricted by context. An important issue in our research is whether indicators of student involvement mean the same thing in different activity settings. For example, are similar levels of student attention in a peer work group in social studies and a recitation in math class likely to have the same correlates and consequences? Involvement and attention can occur for many reasons: interest, challenge, compliance, fear, vigilance, surprise, or sociability, to name a few. The mechanisms behind student involvement must be understood better.

Student involvement is only one of the outcomes of schooling (and a proximal one at that). The demonstration that students directly and systematically respond to educationally significant features of settings must be followed by studies of other consequences. In particular, the relationship between student achievement and experience in different settings should be explored. With achievement information it would be possible to test the assumption that student involvement is a necessary though not sufficient predictor of student learning, and to assess the contributions of setting features to student attainment.

The problem of validly assessing student achievement in two subjects in the context of a correlational study of a wide variety of classes is not easily solved. Standardized achievement tests are not appropriate for the task.[13] Perhaps a good solution would be the use of teacher-made tests and student work samples. Of course, a lack of comparability would still be a problem. The tests could not provide a uniform scale to measure the effectiveness of classroom activities. However, by making comparisons within classes, some insight into student learning would be gained. Methodological advances in psychometrics may also help solve this problem. Alternatively, different research designs would provide ways to surmount some of the difficulties. Nevertheless, the subject matter and curricular differences we have documented suggest that comparability of achievement assessments may not be a realistic goal if curricular validity is also desired.

Intellectual Activity

A very consistent picture of elementary instruction has been produced in previous studies (Dunkin and Biddle 1974; Gage 1978; Jackson 1968; Sirotnik 1983; Goodlad 1984). School children experience heavy doses of teacher talk and low-level intellectual activity. Reporting findings from his large study of schooling, Goodlad (1984) describes pupils as mostly listening to teacher talk or independently practicing skills in classrooms with "flat, neutral emotional ambiance."

This chapter has focused on two interrelated issues: how the learning environment is structured to accomplish certain intellectual purposes, and students' response or involvement in the instructional setting. Do our fifth-grade results look similar to other descriptive studies?

Our data confirm previously documented trends but also show some departures. Both methodological and substantive factors account for the differences. Insufficient attention has been given, even in the most recent studies, to the extent that subject matter, curriculum, and grade level affect classroom practices.

The observation method we used to obtain information about the classroom activity structure was not teacher-centered. Many studies focus on the teacher, deriving a capsule of educational experiences as seen with the teacher at the center. Observations are often restricted to settings in which teacher-student interaction is occurring, because transactions between students and teachers are believed to be the core of teaching (Brophy and Good 1974). But instructional environments have more action structures than teachers talking in front of classes. Our method accounted for the behavior and location of both students and teachers.

The talking teacher as a dominant actor in the classroom did emerge in our aggregate data. About half the math and social studies time was teacher-paced. A teacher running a segment was indeed likely to do a lot of talking. Nevertheless, overall pacing distributions differed by subject and by curricular program, as did the formats used within teacher pacing.

The activity structure approach gives a more complete account of student experience in the classroom. As participants in the curricula described in the last chapter, students in some math classes spent almost all their time in individualized seatwork, with no teacher-led lessons; in other classes, time was more evenly divided between teacher-directed segments (usually recitations and checking work) and seatwork. In social studies the traditional classrooms were dominated by recitations and other teacher-directed activities, but the group-work classes had teacher-paced segments that were mostly preparatory. In group-work classes one rarely saw a recitation.

Previous research found intellectual activity in classrooms impoverished. Our research confirms prior findings when the data are collapsed across all classrooms and the first two levels of the *Taxonomy* (receive/recall facts and learn concepts and skills) are considered low level. In the math classes there is no question that a minute portion of classroom activity was directed toward application—the only higher mental process observed. In social studies, on the other hand, particularly in some group-work classes, a considerably larger portion of student time was spent on developing research skills, application, and other higher mental processes. In fact, research skills were goals in almost every class we studied. As with pacing, we find curricular and subject matter variation here that is not regularly noted by other investigators.

There is, in general, a serious lack of challenging activity in elementary schools. However, the challenging and engaging activity that exists usually takes place when children work together and when students are studying enrichment topics such as social studies as opposed to skill subjects such as mathematics. Since many research protocols involve observation of teacher-directed lessons and/or basic skill subjects, more low-level intellectual activity is likely to be seen than if a sampling of all classroom activities was used.

The asymmetric distribution of cognitive level and pacing partly explains the usually reported findings on intellectual activity. As many prior researchers have examined teacher-directed activities, the predominance of low-level intellectual activities is not surprising and completely consistent with our data. Intellectual impoverishment is likely to be most starkly revealed and most prevalent in teacher-centered studies. Other pacing conditions showed a greater variety of cognitive goals, particularly in social studies.

Why cognitive level varied with pacing condition is a fascinating matter that needs more exploration. The basic question is whether there is an inherent logic to the arrangements we observed. Are the arrangements functionally and pedagogically optimal? For instance, can one justify the fact that most teacher-paced instruction falls at the factual level? Definitive answers cannot be provided without further experimentation and study, but the variety of practice already present in schools suggests that more flexibility and alternative setting structures are viable.

Our analysis of factual segments under teacher direction showed that teachers take charge of certain functions that are not intellectually challenging. In math, checking work is a prime example of an activity that could be handled in other ways in classrooms or outside classroom time.

Checking work seems a poor use of student time except when it provides pupils with needed reinforcement and feedback. Such needs may in fact be met, but more observation would be needed to ascertain the precise value of these activities. As part of their Missouri Mathematics Program, Good and Grouws (1983) have developed homework routines that include feedback and review. Checking work in public may also engender competitive feelings and perceptions of success or failure (Marshall and Weinstein 1984).

One rationale for checking work in a whole-class setting seems to be value to the teacher. A primarily clerical chore that must get done is accomplished, and the teacher obtains some idea of student progress. The activities we coded as checking work are too mechanical to provide diagnostic information to students or teachers, so their primary justification seems to be cutting down on the clerical load that is part of teaching, particularly in basic subjects. Alternative solutions to this burden might be student correction of their work with available answer sheets, correction of work outside class time, or correction of work by the teacher while students are occupied in seatwork.

Work-checking segments may be used primarily for their ritual value. Such activities may help students feel that the classroom environment is predictable. Finally, teachers may conduct such segments as a way to gain some class time during which they can be relatively less active themselves—responding to their need for activities that demand less energy at some point during the long day in the classroom.

Preparatory segments in both math and social studies are another category of low-level work under teacher direction. Transitions and preparatory segments are part of the teacher's management role. The data suggest that preparatory segments in math may be inefficiently executed—the information they contain is often redundant and not needed by most pupils—although teachers may feel obliged to provide these directions for the students who do need them. In social studies, preparatory segments convey information needed for subsequent pupil activities and seem more broadly justified.

A large portion of social studies recitations are at a low level. Although some factual questions are certainly appropriate, teachers' frequently noted deficiency in framing challenging questions was present in our teachers too. Since teachers do conduct some recitations at higher cognitive levels, and students respond with higher involvement, it is important to better understand the curricular contexts that support more complex recitations.

In social studies, child-paced activities reflected the diversity of goals found in most curricula. Pupils were thus assigned independent tasks across the intellectual spectrum, but with some emphasis on research skills, comprehension tasks, and factual knowledge. In the teachers' view, the most suitable activities for pupils on their own are library and other research activities and various writing tasks, including answering textbook or worksheet questions. Logistically, one can see why teachers would most readily ask pupils to do these activities independently, although cooperative efforts would certainly be possible to accomplish such tasks.

The theoretical rationale for the use of cooperative groups in complex problem solving derives from a number of sources reviewed elsewhere (Slavin 1983; Stodolsky 1984a; Graybeal and Stodolsky 1985). Sound arguments can be made to support the use of small groups for complex intellectual purposes, although it is interesting to ask whether teachers themselves have made this pedagogical link or only the developers of special curricula such as *MACOS* and the simulation program seen in Mrs. K.'s class.

The pattern of cognitive level and pacing shows rather clearly the degree to which the teacher as orchestrator and manager of classroom activity carries out functions that are not inherently pedagogical or intellectually complex. But some active teaching, such as recitation, is also directed at low cognitive levels. In a situation that may have parallels in other kinds of managers, the teacher tries to arrange for intellectual activity but often does so by delegating its enactment to children alone or in groups. The teacher's observable behavior, by contrast, is frequently at a lower intellectual level than that expected of the pupils.

There may be a discrepancy between the observable behavior of teachers and their planning and structuring of the classroom. In arranging the classroom activity structure, more complex thinking may also be part of the teacher's repertoire. But an interesting disjunction may exist between the "on-stage" and "off-stage" behavior of teachers. In the classroom, teachers often express more concern with form than with the actual content of instruction because they manage the environment.

Because we used observations of settings in two fields of study, the picture of classroom activity we have drawn is not entirely the same as that developed by other researchers. In a general way, we did find intellectual impoverishment in our classrooms, since most of the activity was limited to cognitive goals at the first two levels of the *Taxonomy*. However, a careful look at our data results in the discovery of a number of important differences.

The distribution of both pacing and cognitive goals differed by subject matter. Considerably more student time was devoted to higher mental processes and research skills in social studies than in math. Similarly, social studies instruction contained more student time in cooperative work groups and under mechanical pacing than math teaching did. The differences resulted in part from program variation *within* subject matters as well as between them.

The asymmetric relationship between pacing and cognitive level reveals that much more low-level intellectual content was found in teacher-run activity than in independent student work or cooperative work, particularly in social studies. Thus the person who is presumably most competent in the educational setting devotes energy to the most mundane activity. This finding also may explain something of an overstatement in other research regarding the extent of intellectual impoverishment in today's classrooms.

Not only is the picture of classroom activity likely to be incomplete in teacher-centered studies, but, as we have shown, the previous findings on correlates of student involvement do not generalize to older students or to settings beyond basic skill subjects. Restricting subject matter and/or focusing solely on teacher behavior or teacher-student interactions has far broader ramifications. Because the organization of instruction varies markedly by subject matter and by who is pacing the activity, the universe of school activity is seriously restricted by those choices. Our data do not include all subjects taught in school, but we went far enough into two very different fields to demonstrate the need for sampling subject matter and program variants before drawing conclusions about how classrooms look and how students react to them.

5

Discussion and Implications

A picture of classroom life has emerged in this study that differs from other portrayals. Our investigation of fifth-grade math and social studies classes highlights the internal variety of the school day, not its sameness. We have found that teachers do not teach in only one way; they alter their instructional approach depending on what they are teaching. Students do not learn in only one way; they are expected to approach mastery of different school subjects through different activities and tasks. When examining classroom activity, the subject matters for teachers and pupils.

We have described subject matter differences, curricular variation, and individual teachers' instructional approaches. Program variants were found in both our subjects, but there was more similarity between math classes than between social studies classes. Also, students' experiences within any math class were very much alike from day to day, whereas more variety was present in most social studies classes.

Our analysis has shown students to be efficient and curious in their responses to features of the setting. The pattern of student involvement revealed a responsive student—one more involved in activities that were complex, entailed collaboration with others, and conveyed novel or needed information, and less involved in activities that were simple, solitary, and characterized by information that was already known, easily surmised, or redundant. Students did not respond to individual teachers in a consistent manner either. At any time, their involvement depended on how the educational setting had been structured.

Many descriptions of schooling have overlooked or glossed over the variety children may experience during a day or week in school. More attention should be paid to the fact that variety occurs and an understanding of its origins, the forces that maintain it, and its consequences.

103

To find variety in school experiences is not to assert that school days comprise highs and lows, rapid changes, and excitement. Much of what we saw in schools was bland, well-regulated, and mediocre. The analysis of segment patterns showed that a very restricted set of possible arrangements actually occurred in classrooms. Some basic institutional verities may dictate that school events be highly routine, but they need not be mindless or boring. We need to find out why teachers rely on such a limited array of instructional forms. Westbury (1978) has discussed this issue in a cogent review of classroom-process research.

GENERALIZABILITY

The documentation of subject-matter differences in instruction seems very solid for the twenty-one teachers we studied in the schools in which they taught. However, the generalizability of the pattern needs to be examined in other teachers and other schools. Our sample was diverse, but not wholly representative of individuals in the teaching force.

The pattern we found—of more similarity in mathematics and more diversity in social studies—probably extends to other basic and enrichment fields. We would expect more instructional time, more uniform topical coverage, more accountability for performance, and less variety in activity structures within and across classes in basic subjects. Others, including Adams and Biddle (1970), Goodlad (1984), Stake and Easley (1978), and Suydam and Osborne (1977), have shown that a field's priority can influence instruction in it.

Although the pattern is probably present in basic and enrichment fields, its generalizability may be muted and limited depending on grade level. In fact, the upper elementary grades, in which we observed, may contain the most pronounced pattern across subjects. In the primary grades, a major part of the instructional day is devoted to language arts and reading, with time for math instruction trailing behind (Weiss 1978; University of Chicago School Mathematics Project 1984). Such enrichment subjects as science, social studies, art, and music are often not taught in the early years or appear sporadically as fillers. In most secondary schools, subjects cannot have varying time slots because fixed periods of instruction are used. Instead, requiring study in a field in high school reflects its priority.

In high school, teacher-dominated lessons, especially recitations and lectures, seem more common in all subjects (Goodlad 1984). However, project work and laboratory exercises involving collaboration are sometimes found in social studies, science, and English classes. Some of the characteristics of activity segments might show subject matter differences at higher grade levels. The cognitive goals addressed in various fields, the types of materials used, and expected student behaviors would be of special interest.

A more extensive look at activities used in various school subjects at a number of grade levels would contribute to a better understanding of the relationship between instruction and subject matter. If there are fundamental constraints on instruction that emanate from the nature of the educational goals or the structure of disciplines, additional data should help us uncover and document their existence. Cross-cultural studies of instruction in a given subject would also suggest how malleable the instructional arrangements are.

ORIGINS OF DIFFERENT ACTIVITY STRUCTURES

So far, the strongest and most detailed case has been made for the impact on instruction of subject matter, along with specific curricular programs and topics. Here we probe some related issues further and examine, at least briefly, other factors that may also contribute to the creation of particular instructional arrangements. In the process, a research agenda for the future will be described.

Community Influences

Although they have not been central to this research, distal factors, such as community characteristics and school district expenditures, may influence the creation and use of certain instructional arrangements. Thomas and Kemmerer (1983) examined the allocation of educational resources between homes and schools, as well as the role of school expenditures and the social status of districts in shaping classroom instruction. Their sample was larger than ours but included our schools. They found systematic variation in instructional practices and course offerings, depending on parental educational and occupational levels. For example, higher-status schools tended to offer broader curricula, including such subjects as music and art. Within mathematics, individualized instruction and procedures involving less than the whole class were found more often in higher-SES districts. They found no association between instructional arrangements and SES in social studies classes.

In the data we analyzed, no strong associations were found between types of instructional arrangements and demographic characteristics of districts. However, there is a slight suggestion that certain activity setting features are curvilinear in their distribution across SES levels. Small-group work in social studies and individualized mathematics programs were slightly more likely to be found in our low- and high-SES districts than in middle-SES districts. These trends should be investigated further.

Thomas and Kemmerer (1983) found instructional differentiation to be associated with differential distribution of resources, such as books, textbooks, and square feet per pupil. They believe both the types of materials and their quantity and quality affect teachers' ability to instruct. Where resources are scarce, instructional options may be limited. However, materials on the shelf are not guaranteed use in classrooms.

Swings of public opinion can influence activities in classrooms. Public concern is sometimes translated into legislation or district policies. One example is the "back-to-basics" movement, which led to the passage, by more than thirty states, of laws mandating minimum competency testing (Pipho 1977). Another example is career education, which is required in elementary schools in Illinois.

The instructional philosophy of a school may also influence classroom procedures. Schools set policy to ensure content coverage or to support certain pedagogical approaches (e.g., open education, individualization). Overall, it was difficult for our observers to predict the form of an instructional program with knowledge of district characteristics alone. However, the influence of school philosophy was very evident in the ways classrooms and school life were organized in some schools. For instance, the school in which we observed teachers L and M adhered to a progressive philosophy that had been present in the district since after World War I. The social studies curriculum was organized around cooperative work groups and used *MACOS*. Math classes followed a program developed by the district, including ways to individualize instruction. Another school, in which we observed Mr. Q., had adopted a back-to-basics approach, coupled with a strong discipline and homework policy. In this traditional school, classrooms in both subjects were organized around whole-class instruction and emphasized textbook coverage. The latter district was most concerned with products of learning, not the process, whereas the reverse was true in the progressive district.

Certain milieu effects were evident to those of us who spent time in the schools. Ferguson (1984) has shown that teachers were more frequently delegated authority to choose curricula and work out class assignments and grouping arrangements in our upper-SES districts. She believes that giving teachers autonomy will result in more effective instruction and use of resources.

Although some of our schools had a fairly uniform school philosophy and curricular commitments, in others these features were not clearly evident. Within-school consistency can be studied by comparing programs and activity patterns for teachers at the same school. We have not conducted such an analysis of specific segment features, but different curricular programs were operating in the same school and the same subject matter in a number of sample schools, while a uniform curriculum was followed in others. State and local authorities attempt to control what is taught and how much time is allocated to particular subjects with curricular guidelines. In some school districts, teachers all work with the same materials, while in others they have considerable discretion in choice of materials and programs of study.

Students

The contribution of student characteristics to instructional decisions and practices will receive only passing mention. There is an extensive literature on how different students react to or benefit from various instructional approaches. For example, comparisons of the classroom behavior of boys and girls, or of students having differing abilities, have been frequent. The problem of accommodating individual students has also produced a voluminous literature of applied and conceptual research.

The composition of a class, often established by school tracking policies, determines the degree and type of student heterogeneity with which a teacher must work. Exactly how class composition affects teachers' instructional practices has been investigated by Barr and Dreeben (1983) with respect to the creation of reading groups in first-grade classes. In addition to ability distributions, sex composition and other features of classroom groups might be investigated to see if they influence the way in which instruction is arranged.

Of course instructional procedures are affected by children's grade level and age. Teachers must consider an activity's psychological and developmental appropriateness. Lengths of instructional periods, reliance on the written word as opposed to speaking or direct action, and other features of instruction vary with grade level. The inclusion of a school subject in students' programs is determined by grade level, too.

Tests—Accountability

School and district policies are sometimes enacted by establishing standards to be met by students and/or faculty. Programs of student testing greatly influence what is taught. In most schools, external tests establish subject-matter priorities even if that function is not intended. The school curriculum is at times reduced to instruction that matches the content of standardized tests or other external assessment procedures.

The preoccupation of teachers and students with adequate performance on standardized tests tends to make standards once thought of as minimal the ends of the educational enterprise. In most elementary schools, pressures from standardized tests are directly applied only in basic subjects. However, the existence of assessments in the basics limits the classroom time given to other subjects, as is evident in our data on instructional time and timing of lessons in math and social studies.

In many schools, instruction is derailed in order to "prepare" students for standardized tests. Sessions devoted to reviewing content expected on tests and to practicing with test formats are common. These activities occur under considerable pressure and concern that students perform acceptably; however, they ordinarily do not fit with an orderly plan for instruction in the subject. The dislocation to students and teachers caused by preparation for external exams is often severe, and instructional momentum is sometimes lost for the rest of the school year.

Efforts to have students perform adequately on standardized tests would not be highly negative if the learning goals that resulted were desirable. Unfortunately, at least at the elementary school level, there is an unequivocal emphasis on factual information and basic skills, with little or no emphasis on concept attainment, application, problem solving, or other higher mental processes (Haney 1984). In a revealing article on the history of standardized testing, Buros (1977) documents the trend toward fractionated and lower-mental-process questions in tests. Test item formats—

almost always variants of the multiple-choice type—encourage learning and test-taking strategies focused on recognizing right answers. The actual production of communication—for example, written or oral statements that contain consecutive sentences and thoughts—is not required in most testing situations. Expressions of opinions, values, or points of view are also outside the realm of the test-preparation mentality.

Partly as a consequence of testing, but also due to the perceived importance of the subjects, concern about pupil achievement is endemic in basic fields. The problem of individual differences in learning is conceptualized differently in math and social studies, and possibly in other basic and enrichment fields. Individual differences in learning or learning rates are addressed more programmatically in math, yet uniform goals for learning are often assumed in enrichment areas such as social studies. However, a lack of attainment is treated with less obvious pedagogical response in social studies than in math. Individualization, remediation, enrichment, and programs for talented and gifted children all occur more frequently in math. Such efforts are responses to a mandate for individual mastery and learning.

Pressure for student attainment in math may be one reason teachers do not consider joint efforts appropriate for serious learning in the subject. Of course, teachers may also believe that the structure and sequence of mathematics requires a more fixed approach. Whereas groups of children work together on complex tasks in social studies, in math face-to-face groups are usually formed only to play games with less complex goals (Graybeal and Stodolsky 1985). We infer that teachers do not think group work is an effective way to attain individual mastery of mathematics, although there are data to contradict that belief (Davidson 1980; Sharan et al. 1980; Slavin, Leavey, and Madden 1984). Of course, a stated goal for social studies is developing awareness and consideration of others. Classroom conditions in which children learn to cooperate are a very direct pedagogical embodiment of desired social studies goals.

Lack of accountability pressures contributes to the diversity we saw in social studies. Long-standing progressive ideals, such as those espoused by Dewey, more often find expression in social studies than in math. Math is approached within a restricted cognitive range, with little concrete or manipulative experience for children, with little use of peer interaction, and with no student options in the learning process. Many social studies classes include more cognitively complex goals, sometimes make extensive use of peer learning, and provide more variety in materials and experiences for pupils. Even in social studies, however, few activity options are available to students beyond the possible selection of a topic within an otherwise prescribed project or assignment. Teachers do not act as if they believe ten-year-olds will make appropriate activity choices in educational settings, although in some cases giving children activity options might prove rewarding.

Textbooks

In our earlier discussions of subject matter differences in instruction, insufficient emphasis may have been given to the role of textbooks in determining educational practices. Surprisingly, though textbooks are present in most elementary classrooms, only a few studies have examined the exact ways they are used. Clark and Yinger (1979) found that materials at hand, such as textbooks and teacher's guides, were used by teachers in selecting topics and in sequencing content. Durkin (1984) observed reading lessons of sixteen teachers to see how instruction matched recommended procedures in teacher's manuals. She found conformity only with certain types of suggestions, such as the use of assessment questions. Other suggested practices, such as developing new vocabulary through context, were not consistently adopted. With respect to the use of math textbooks, Schwille et al. (1983) conducted seven case studies of fourth-grade teachers and found that different teachers using the same math textbook or program did not teach identical content. Some teachers followed the books very closely, while others were quite selective.

Krammer (1985) compared teaching practices of eighth-grade mathematics teachers in The Netherlands who were using three different textbooks. He used teachers' reports of their practices and some classrooms observation data to see if different books were associated with different teaching behaviors. Overall, teachers with a textbook that emphasized higher-order questions did ask more such questions than other teachers. Those using a book that emphasized student practice used more seatwork activities. As Krammer notes, it is not clear whether the congruence of textbook content and teacher practices arose because the teachers followed the book or because the teachers selected books that matched their pedagogical styles. Nevertheless, this type of investigation could be usefully extended.

Floden et al. (1981) did a simulation study of teachers' decisions about content in mathematics. When the textbook, published test results, and objectives were compared as influences on math content, teachers perceived the textbook as least powerful. However, it is not known to what extent the simulation situation reflects decisions teachers usually make.

Schwille et al. (1983) suggest that math textbooks and workbooks tend to place a cap on content coverage, a conclusion that is consistent with our observations in math classes too. Everything in textbooks was not used by the math teachers we observed. Introductory examples or material were often omitted. We also saw teachers assign only some of the problems in the book. In giving pupils assignments they omitted word problems and other application exercises, as well as exercises that seemed redundant. Teachers also made materials or used commercially available materials related to topics under study. But topics not included in the books were rarely introduced and the books' ordering of chapters was usually retained.

It is more difficult to formulate a generalization about content coverage and textbooks in social studies. Certain of the teachers we observed stayed very close to textbook content, but others used a variety of materials in addition to or instead of textbooks. Goodlad (1984) asserts that textbooks are preeminent in elementary school math and language arts, but more varied materials are used in social studies. His conclusions seem consistent with our observations.

Closer to the general concerns of this book is the question of what pedagogical practices are actually suggested in teachers' guides, how they differ by subject, and whether teachers follow them. In a project in progress (Graybeal and Stodolsky 1986; Graybeal and Stodolsky 1987; Graybeal, in preparation), we are analyzing ten teachers' guides that accompany the most widely used fifth-grade math and social studies textbooks. We have focused on the recommendations for instructional arrangements and classroom activities by coding many of the activity segment features previously observed in classrooms. In both subjects, very traditional practices are recommended. For example, almost all suggested activities involve the entire class; only 4 percent suggest use of peer work groups. Instructional formats are also weighted toward recitation, other teacher presentations, and seatwork. However, textbook writers communicate distinct pedagogical information to teachers within and across the two subjects.

Of interest is that some social studies series recommend the use of discussion and student reports, whereas some math guides suggest demonstrations, games, and checking work. These formats are recommended primarily in just one of the subjects. From what we saw, there is a general correspondence between recommendations in the guides and classroom practice, but there are some obvious departures too. For instance, in social studies classes we observed much less discussion than recommended, with recitation used instead. We also found more audiovisual activities in social studies than were recommended in the texts. On the other hand, math teachers did fewer demonstrations and made less use of games than suggested in the manuals.

In our observations, the variety of cognitive levels addressed in social studies classes mirrors rather closely the levels of activities suggested by teachers' guides. In math, learning concepts and skills received the most emphasis both in manuals and in classrooms. However, the math guides recommended more work than was actually done in application, symbolic research skills, and other assignments requiring higher mental processes. About 15 percent of suggested math activities were at levels above concepts and skills, but we only observed about 3 percent of segments at those higher levels. Nicely (1985) in an analysis of the treatment of complex numbers in math textbooks for grades three to six, also estimated that higher order processes were demanded around 10 to 15 percent of the time, a proportion he considered far too low.

The manuals suggest different types of activities in math and social studies as reflected in suggested student behaviors as well as format and cognitive level. There are also differences within a subject, depending on the series analyzed. Thus both textbooks in a given subject and specific textbooks within subjects contain distinctive pedagogical suggestions. We intend to further examine the issue of textbook use and to look in more detail at the ways in which our teachers and others conform to suggested practices. Clearly, more systematic information about how teachers use textbooks and teachers' guides is needed. Although the almost universal presence of textbooks in elementary schools is well documented, their classroom use needs much more attention. More specifically, the extent to which teachers follow suggested procedures in teachers' guides and adhere to textbook order and questions needs study. Squire (1987) provides a review of research on textbooks and suggests future investigations.

Textbooks are not always an educational asset. They present serious problems in format and content. Armbruster (1984) has shown that many social studies textbooks are limited in that their questions focus on details rather than comprehension of main ideas. She has also documented a lack of structural coherence in written materials in social studies that make conceptual learning and comprehension difficult for students. Mosenthal (1983) has found that social studies and science textbooks often make unwarranted assumptions about children's knowledge of concepts, making comprehension of text difficult.

The frequent practice in math of teaching a skill, providing practice with that skill in a predictable problem format, and then going on to another one is a procedure that almost guarantees forgetting and lack of connected learning. Students often learn that "this page has problems to be done with this procedure" but do not develop a conceptual understanding that they can use in new situations. In general discussions of task form and its effects, others (Blumenfeld, Mergendoller, and Swarthout 1987; Posner 1982) suggest some reasons that existing math text designs create learning difficulties. Usiskin et al. (1986) are attempting to correct the problem by the use of spaced and mixed practice of problem types in the high school mathematics textbooks they are producing.

Teachers

Teachers' own preferences and values influence the way they structure classroom activity (Bussis, Chittenden, and Amarel 1976). Among other work, Plihal's (1982) is interesting since she found an association between student involvement and teachers' reward orientations and preferences. (Her sample included the teachers we studied and others.) Plihal asked teachers to indicate their subject matter preferences and the rewards they perceived in teaching. Their responses suggest a modest relationship between preferences, reward orientation, and actual teaching practice. Teachers who most valued the direct experience of working with students used activities, such as group work in social studies, that allowed children to be more active participants in the classroom. Teachers who valued achievement as the primary reward of teaching tended to have social studies classes in which pupils were more passive. Further, teachers who found teaching rewarding in itself had social studies classrooms with higher student involvement than teachers who placed more value on achievement outcomes.

Past experience enters into teachers' decisions about instructional practices. A teacher who has tried a particular instructional arrangement—for example, peer work groups—will make an assessment of its success. The teacher may see the arrangement as successful or unsuccessful in terms of student learning or attitudes, as demanding too much work or preparation, as useful for some children but not others; the teacher may find that colleagues object to the increased noise level. Such considerations alter the probability that the teacher would use a given instructional arrangement again. They also contribute to the teacher's view of the applicability and desirability of the particular approach.

Past experiences as reflected in the repertoire of skills, abilities, and knowledge the teacher has mastered also influence decisions about instructional arrangements. Knowledge of certain tasks and topics affects the teacher's selection of both instructional form and instructional content. Teachers' knowledge of subject matter is an important part of their contribution to instruction. Do differing levels or types of teacher competence in a school subject influence instruction; and if they do, what processes are involved? Shulman (1986) and his colleagues are collecting "intellectual histories" from graduate students who are preparing to be secondary school teachers as one approach to these questions. They will attempt to link factors in prospective teachers' background and prior learning to their teaching decisions and behaviors, with particular emphasis on teachers' knowledge and use of subject matter. In a complementary vein, Leinhardt (1983), using a cognitive psychology approach, is carefully mapping teachers' instruction in mathematics with respect to specific aspects of subject matter.

The training teachers receive about pedagogy in specific school subjects is worthy of more study. An analysis of books used in teacher-training courses will be one contribution to this area (Stodolsky 1986). It would also be interesting to know more about the pedagogical beliefs of trainers of teachers in different fields of study. Feiman-Nemser (1983) reviewed what is known about learning to teach. One of her conclusions was that informal influences are more powerful than formal courses and teacher preparation exercises in shaping how teachers teach. Her review demonstrates the need for much more systematic inquiry in this nascent field of teacher development and teacher education. Our research suggests that variations in teachers' instructional repertoires should be examined in studies of teacher development.

Investigators are showing greater interest in the mental life of teachers. Knowledge about how teachers decide what to teach and how they plan instruction is being gathered (e.g., Schwille et al. 1983; Clark and Yinger 1979; Clark and Peterson 1986; Shavelson and Stern 1981; Elbaz 1983). We did not obtain information from our teachers about the connections between their classroom instruction and their past experiences and values. An obvious follow-up of our research would involve interviews with teachers to obtain their views of why they teach each subject as they do. Interviews in conjunction with systematic observations of specific teacher's classrooms would be especially desirable.

Content and Topics

A fundamental question that arises from our findings is the extent to which particular educational goals require certain pedagogical means. The question gains more substance, and perhaps nuance, from the finding that there were no content distinctions in the two program variants in math but rather clear content distinctions in the program variants in social studies.

In social studies, there seems to be a connection between disciplinary origins of topics, cognitive goals, and classroom activities. Recall that topics from psychology and anthropology tended to appear in group-work classes, while history and geography were more likely to be found in teacher-centered classes. Furthermore, complex intellectual goals such as higher mental processes and application were more likely to be addressed in the group-work programs than in the traditional ones, although research skills were taught in both.

It could be argued that disciplinary alignment with anthropology, sociology, and psychology results in heightened concern for interpersonal processes in the classroom and leads to social studies programs with small-group problem solving and higher mental processes as goals of instruction. A pedagogical assertion that small groups facilitate complex problem solving may also be involved.

We may actually be seeing a legacy of the progressive education movement which, in some ways, invented social studies as an interdisciplinary school subject. The progressives emphasized cooperative learning among pupils as well as subject matter integration and problem solving. Our group-work classes often had those characteristics.

One way to account for the teacher-centered approach in history

CARNEGIE LIBRARY
LIVINGSTONE COLLEGE
SALISBURY, NC 28144

and geography is that these fields are more structured or ordered than other content included in social studies programs. Perhaps traditional forms of teaching are more regularly found in sequential subjects; we certainly found that pattern in math. A possible emphasis on a body of knowledge to be mastered in history and geography may also incline teachers to instruct in a traditional fashion. On the other hand, the flexibility of content coverage in other aspects of social studies, indeed the arbitrariness and fuzziness, may permit or encourage a broader range of instructional arrangements.

Even if the ordered and somewhat sequential nature of history and geography contributes to the use of teacher-centered instruction, it does not seem an entirely satisfactory explanation for the relative lack of emphasis on problem solving and higher mental processes in the traditional classes. In this arena, it is more likely that the conception of these subjects as collections of facts to be learned influences the cognitive goals of instruction.

At a much more general level, Grannis (1975) has proposed that certain settings are optimal for achieving the goals of community, competence, and individuation. His theoretical analysis might provide a starting point for inquiry on instruction that develops a variety of intellectual and social processes in students.

Another approach to the question of pedagogy and content would be examination of various curricular practices found for a given topic or unit. An understanding of the variety of ways a given topic is taught might provide some insights into the constraints that apply to instruction in specific subject matter. Cognitive psychologists are increasingly claiming that learning is subject specific (e.g., Carey 1985) and teaching may be too.

A related type of investigation would involve cross-cultural comparisons of textbooks and instructional methods. Stigler, Lee, Lucker, and Stevenson (1982) and Stigler, Fuson, Ham, and Kim (1986) have examined mathematics instruction in the United States, Japan, and China, and textbooks from the United States and the Soviet Union. They have found marked differences in the organization of content, the type of content covered, and actual instructional practices across countries. The first IEA study (Husen 1967) provided data about mathematics instruction in a number of countries and has been followed by research on instruction and achievement in other subjects (e.g., Walker 1976). Cross-national comparisons help us understand the variety of ways the same content can be taught.

Last, more historical and conceptual analysis of how subjects came into the school curriculum and the values they were meant to serve might provide a rather different approach to understanding how instruction came to look the way it does in certain subjects. The roots of certain traditions of teaching should be better understood. In this vein, Jackson (1986) has made a useful distinction between mimetic and transformative traditions of teaching and learning and has traced some of their origins.

The demonstration of subject matter and curricular variation in classroom activity has suggested an extended agenda of research on the origins of classroom activity. Questions range from the influence of such distal variables as community characteristics to factors such as the impacts of textbooks and teachers' training on instructional arrangements. Special attention should be paid to what is being taught as these issues are pursued, so that we may better understand why classroom instruction looks the way it does.

THE MEANING OF LEARNING

The *form* of instructional settings in which children work produces *knowledge about learning* along with planned achievements. Children do not only learn the content of lessons. They also learn what it means to learn. The impact of experiences on peoples' values and meaning systems has been discussed by many social scientists (e. g., Berger and Luckmann 1966; Breer and Locke 1965; Dreeben 1968; Goffman 1959; Kluckhohn 1961; Marton and Saljo 1976; Mead 1934). It is assumed that experiences, especially repetitive ones such as classroom activities, have both explicit and implicit meanings for the participants.

The implicit, hidden curriculum is a set of values, messages, and meanings that are transmitted through school experience even though their transmission is not explicitly planned (Dreeben 1968; Jackson 1968). Much implicit learning occurs in the daily interactions between teachers and children and in their physical and social milieu. It is posited that daily experiences have their effect through a variety of mechanisms, including direct learning and rehearsal as well as less conscious mechanisms that are characteristic of many socialization experiences. Among the processes that may be involved are identification, modeling, and conditioning.

Emphasis must also be placed on the active role participants play in the construction of meaning. Traditions of inquiry that are rooted in anthropology, history, and social psychology are being applied in a variety of social sciences including studies in education (Erickson 1986; Shulman 1986). Such research confirms that students actively interpret their school experiences in light of their own expectations, histories, and needs as well as the objective conditions they encounter. For all these reasons, we believe that pupils will develop conceptions of how one learns various subjects, and be more or less disposed to learn each of them, in response to their experience with instruction in different school subjects.

For example, if teachers always introduce new material and concepts to children, this may result in children's assuming (not necessarily consciously) that adult explanation is a necessary part of learning in that curricular area. On the other hand, the utilization of written resources, television, or computers could produce different conceptions of the learning process, including whether a particular subject is seen as easy or hard to learn (Salomon 1983). Students in schools that rely on essay exams rather than multiple-choice tests (Madaus, Airasian, and Kellaghan 1980) develop different views of learning and content mastery, much as occurs when learning sets are induced (Luchins 1942).

While participating in a given instructional and task structure, pupils learn how to function within the particular task or activity form. Presumably, experience with recitation, peer work groups, tutoring, or seatwork facilitates future student performance in similar settings (cf. Anderson, Brubaker, Alleman-Brooks, and Duffy 1985). Thus, children learn to do worksheets or to write essays and in the process absorb information both about the content of a particular assignment and about the way they are to set up a page, how to use time, what the teacher is likely to expect as a product, etc.

Particular formats require particular skills if participation in them is to be effective (Blumenfeld, Mergendoller, and Swarthout 1987; Doyle 1983; Posner 1982). There are at least two aspects to successful task performance. One is knowledge about the actual content of the task and prerequisite skills and abilities; good instructional practice usually addresses this need. The other is a set of skills (one is tempted to say *metaskills*) that involve knowing how to do the task *qua* task. Children are rarely given explicit instruction in this domain but perforce develop varying levels of skill in it. For various activities and tasks, there are prerequisites in both task content and task procedure. Greeno (1978) demonstrated that students must know certain patterns of solution in order to succeed in geometry problem solving, and that the necessary patterns are rarely explicitly taught. Schoenfeld (1983) has also examined how students' beliefs and metacognitions influence mathematical problem solving in the area of plane geometry. Both researchers showed that problem solutions require not only specific content knowledge but beliefs which allow students to use or abandon certain strategies during problem solving. For instance, Schoenfeld found his students held certain beliefs about what mathematical behavior really was that interfered with their ability to solve the geometry problems given them. He also found that students working in pairs avoided some of the least productive strategies (e.g., staying with one line of proof too long) used by students who worked alone.

Tobias (1982) provides another example in his discussion of macroprocesses, such as review, note taking, and various other mechanisms for averting confusion that students use as they work with instructional materials. He suggested that different instructional approaches may lead students to employ differing repertoires of macroprocesses, and when this is the case, differences in learning would be expected. Although Tobias's work is in its early stages, it contains heuristically useful ideas that are consistent with those underlying this discussion.

Activities in small groups provide another area to consider. When students engage in group problem solving or other collaborative tasks, they must be able to work together effectively in addition to having needed content knowledge (Stodolsky 1984a). As Slavin (1983) has shown, specific strategies or group-work structures are needed. For instance, delegation of parts of the task to individuals or the selection of a leader may be effective ways for a particular group to accomplish its assigned task. Group settings are thus another case in which both task form and content must be mastered.

To return to our general point, as students learn content and ways of functioning within instructional forms, they also learn the *meaning of learning* as defined in their educational environment. The impact of task form and content on children's ideas about learning is multifaceted. For example, task experiences might affect children's interests, their assessments of the ease of learning in a particular area, and conditions or resources thought necessary for learning. Another set of activities and tasks may convey different conceptions of how one goes about being an effective learner.

There is an extensive literature on possible connections between properties of the learning environment and different types of learning. The direct outcomes of instruction are not the central focus in the present discussion. Obviously instructional arrangements contribute to the planned achievements of students. Academic (cognitive) learning is usually emphasized, but sometimes the teacher has explicit objectives in the affective, social, moral, and physical domains. That instruction planned for one purpose has other consequences is a fact that needs underlining. Instructional decisions that lead to classroom practices for achieving cognitive goals may simultaneously produce social, attitudinal, emotional, and other effects. Conversely, classroom activities planned for social or affective goals also have cognitive and other consequences.

Some analysts have focused on the messages conveyed to students in schools about good behavior, cooperation, competition, social status, and how to get good grades. Doyle (1977, 1983) described the activity structure as a setting for a performance-grade exchange. Blumenfeld et al. (1982) postulated a role for classroom context in the development of self-perceptions of ability. Rosenholtz and Wilson (1980) found that children's self-perceptions differed in highly individualized and traditional classrooms, with more consensus regarding pupils' abilities in traditional classes. Bossert (1979) found a similar influence of classroom organization on students' sociometric ratings.

Other researchers (Minuchin et al. 1969; Horwitz 1979; Shapiro 1973) have examined consequences of differing curricular arrangements, particularly informal (open) and traditional programs. Horwitz (1979) reviewed the effects of open education on children's achievement, self-concepts, creativity, locus of control, and attitudes. His conclusion, confirmed in a research synthesis by Giaconia and Hedges (1982), is that children in open environments exhibit more positive self-concepts and are more creative than those in programs in which activity is specified by the teacher and the same for all pupils. Activity choice seems to be the mechanism that produces such outcomes. Children select activities, presumably following their interests and abilities, and a wider range of behavior is acceptable in open environments. Such classrooms offer many more activities through which a child can develop self-esteem than are found in traditional classrooms.

Educational researchers are beginning to document the broader impact of educational settings on children's learning, behaviors, and attitudes. The daily experiences of children in different settings appear to have differing psychic consequences. In particular, we are interested in the ways in which task experiences produce perceptions of what it means to learn, how to accomplish tasks, and how to evaluate oneself and others. While existing data in these areas are limited, they are rather consistent. Further inquiry should ask questions such as: How is this classroom experience shaping children's ways of learning? What does it mean to be a successful or effective learner in this classroom? How does one learn mathematics? What is easy in this classroom? What is hard? Who is valued in this environment?

In the long run, it may be more important to understand how children develop ways of learning and approaches to new learning than to understand the specifics of what they have learned at a given time. Specific content is rather quickly forgotten, but ideas about how and whether to learn something endure. Much of the significance of studying classroom activity arises from its role in shaping behaviors, beliefs, attitudes, and perceptions in students and teachers. Schooling as planned is meant to affect and change its participants, but many of its unplanned results also need to be documented.

Routes to Learning

If educational environments have unplanned results, what are the consequences of subject matter differences in instructional activity? Here we explore the effects on students of having specific classroom arrangements tied to particular school subjects. As we have just suggested in general terms, we presume that students will associate certain ways of learning with different subjects. Over time, classroom experiences should shape students' ideas about routes to learning, interests, and attitudes.

Various routes to learning may be available to students in elementary school classrooms. They include: teachers' explanations of new concepts and procedures; written materials that explain new concepts and procedures and provide information; graphic symbolic materials, including maps, that can be used to obtain information;

audiovisual materials that convey information; exercises with manipulatives and concrete objects that provide a basis for understanding concepts, for discovery of relationships, or for solving problems; face-to-face interaction with peers to collaborate in problem solving or discussion; obtaining help from another student in a tutorial relationship or informally; and obtaining help from the teacher.

Our observations in math and social studies documented many differences in the ways students go about learning in the two subjects. If one thinks about the two activity patterns in terms of the routes to learning they provide, a striking contrast becomes evident.

Within the traditional math programs, very few of the potential routes to learning we listed were available to students. Basically, the teacher and textbooks were the major, and usually the only, resources to which students had regular access in math classes. If students wanted to find out what something meant or how to do something, or to learn whether their work was acceptable or correct, teachers and textbooks were about the only places to turn.

Since textbooks may play a very significant role for students, we coded them as part of the variable feedback. For that purpose, we ascertained whether the books provided explanations that students could use on their own and whether they provided answers to questions posed or means to verify answers, such as self-checking routines. We also looked at the overall structure of the textbooks in the two subjects, at the way we saw them used, and research that deals with their use. Of course, math and social studies books are unalike in structure, but their main features are worth considering.

Math textbooks at this grade level are little more than collections of problem sets. They contain limited examples and little in the way of explanatory material to aid conceptual understanding. A student who needed to learn a principle or new algorithm would ordinarily not find enough developmental material in a textbook to be likely to succeed using the book alone. At best, concepts or algorithms are presented incompletely, usually by giving one or two illustrative problems or providing hints and reminders.

The limited utility of the math textbooks for autonomous learning is confirmed in a study by the National Advisory Committee on Mathematical Education (1975). In describing elementary school math classes, the study concludes: "The text is followed fairly closely, but students are likely to read at most one or two pages out of five pages of textual materials other than problems. It seems likely that the text, at least as far as the students are concerned, is primarily a source of problem lists" (p. 77). Students do not tend to use math texts independently, and they are not regularly directed to use the textual materials that are not problem sets. Our classes generally followed the pattern found nationally.

Social studies texts contain primarily narrative material, accompanied by pictures, maps, and graphs. Questions appear in the textbooks at the end of chapters or sections, and they are sometimes interspersed in the text. Armbruster (1984) discusses features of textbook materials that promote learning of important information. In Armbruster's view, the coherence and structure of the text and the use of various signaling devices are associated with student recall and comprehension. She found some social studies books very adequate for student comprehension and others deficient. Our inspection of social studies textbooks showed that it is possible to obtain information from them, especially the information required to answer the questions posed by the text authors. Armbruster (1984) analyzed a small number of textbook units for fifth-grade social studies and concluded that most of the questions directed students to details rather than to main ideas. Even though the content and questions in many social studies textbooks are certainly not ideal, the information required to answer the questions is present in the books.[1]

A broadly accepted assumption about how to teach math in elementary school became apparent when we combined knowledge of the textbooks with our observations of classroom instruction. Math teachers are expected to present new material and explain how to do problems. Math textbooks do not systematically attend to developing conceptual understanding in pupils. Textbooks are meant to be used in conjunction with teacher instruction and explanation. Except in the individualized programs in which students obtain almost all instruction from sequenced materials, children learning math are not expected to do so without initial teacher guidance and explanation. Traditional math instruction places all but the exceptional student in a position of almost total dependence on the teacher for progress through a course.

In essence, the traditional math classes contain only one route to learning: teacher presentation of concepts followed by independent student practice. This protocol is usually found in elementary schools (Stake and Easley 1978; Goodlad 1984; Fey 1979). When students are asked to describe their math classroom experiences, they characterize their time as spent in "listening to and watching the teacher do mathematics" and in solving problems on their own (Carpenter et al. 1981, p. 136).

Whereas teachers seem to have almost exclusive responsibility for introducing new material in math, the situation is very different in social studies. An explicit goal of most social studies programs is to help students become independent learners, and especially to develop research skills. The development of research skills was the one cognitive goal that appeared in almost every class we observed. Regardless of the type of social studies program, students were expected to gather information from a variety of sources, including textbooks, reference books, maps, globes, and newspapers. Reading to acquire information and to learn new concepts and ideas was an integral part of social studies instruction.

Our observations suggest a considerable range in the degree to which pupils succeed in mastering research skills and other tactics that facilitate independent learning. Students are often guided with questions (posed by teachers or textbooks) prior to a research or reading exercise, or they are questioned afterward. Our impression is that fifth graders are being exposed to skills that will help them learn independently, but in many classrooms they are not yet very adept. Nevertheless, the social studies classes seem to provide more basis for student autonomy and more possible ways to learn than the math classes.

Many more of the possible routes to learning are available to students in social studies classes than in math classes. Even in traditional, teacher-led classes, the textbooks provide necessary, if sometimes banal, information and concepts to students, and training in research skills is a part of the curricular program. In traditional social studies classes, pupils have regular access to reference materials, including maps and encyclopedias; films and film strips; and textbooks and the teacher. In group-work classes, students gain experience with many routes to learning including collaboration and discussion with other pupils, the use of written and symbolic materials in libraries and classrooms, textbooks or other curricular materials, and the teacher.

Elsewhere (Stodolsky 1985) a case has been developed to connect instructional procedures in math classes to the development of negative attitudes toward math and math aversion in children, adolescents, and adults. The argument, briefly reviewed here, illustrates the type of analysis that might be effectively applied to other teaching and learning settings.

We have conjectured that negative attitudes toward math and a ready acceptance of ability as the prime determinant of math achievement follow from long exposure to a limited instructional approach. Math students' textbooks are noninstructional. Students do not have concrete objects or manipulatives, and cooperative learning is not used in their classrooms. Students are conditioned over many years to rely on the teacher: they expect to be "told" math (Stodolsky 1985). If the teacher's explanation is inadequate or unavailable, students have little recourse to other avenues for learning and almost no awareness that other strategies are available. As a consequence, many come to believe they simply lack the ability to learn. In fact, Hoyles (1982) has found that students have stronger ideas about their math abilities (or inabilities) than they do about their abilities in other subjects.

Since most social studies classrooms provide students with a number of ways to learn, we expect that pupils would feel capable of learning social studies if they were interested in doing so. Even with incomplete mastery of research skills, it seems plausible that pupils would think themselves able to pursue new ideas or lines of investigation in social studies, whereas this expectation would be less likely in math. We would suppose that social studies pupils believe they have more places to turn to achieve learning goals and can take more personal responsibility for learning. In interviews about math and social studies with a small number of children, Glaessner (1986) has found differences in the extent to which pupils believe they can learn each subject on their own. Students voice more autonomy in discussing social studies than they do regarding math. Glaessner also found that students seem to view social studies instruction as more permeable and open to change than math instruction.[2]

In general, students' views of the routes or opportunities they can use in learning are an important set of outcomes associated with classroom instruction. Whether a student believes that independent learning in a field is possible, that he or she can "figure it out," is an important part of the meaning attached to learning. Similarly, the view that adults and other students are possible sources of help or collaborators is another pivotal factor in student conceptions. The need for adult explanation in new learning, as distinguished from the possibility of autonomous learning, may be another important dimension along which students' ideas about learning differ. Such student ideas are probably influenced by their school experiences in learning different school subjects.

Student Attitudes

There is little direct evidence to connect classroom experiences and students' attitudes and perceptions. But there are data regarding students' attitudes towards school subjects, which we now examine for their consistency with our general theme. Goodlad (1984), Brush (1980), and the National Assessment of Educational Progress (Carpenter et al. 1981) had elementary and high school students rank subjects by how much they liked them, their perceived difficulty, and their importance. An intriguing pattern can be seen in the data.

On the average, students like math and science in the elementary grades, but they dislike both subjects more in junior high and high school. As their dislike increases, so does their judgment of the subjects' difficulty. Thus ratings of difficulty and dislike go hand in hand in science and math and increase through the school years, with a dramatic change of valence in junior high. A concomitant belief that ability plays a critical role in learning math is also part of this picture.

Social studies shows a different pattern (Goodlad 1984). The field is not well liked across the grades, but students do not report finding it difficult. In fact, most students rate social studies as "easy" or "just right" through the school grades. If anything, many students find social studies lacks challenge; it is boring.

The picture for English is not entirely consistent. Both Brush (1980) and Goodlad (1984) found that students in high school liked English better than they did in junior high, and it was at the top of the list in Brush's study. Goodlad's respondents ranked it best liked among traditional academic subjects, but below arts, vocational education, and physical education. The results are slightly equivocal on the perceived difficulty of English. Either students' ratings do not change through the grades or pupils see English as slightly easier in high school. In this case, difficulty and dislike do not seem closely linked.

Last, foreign language was ranked the least liked subject at all grades in Goodlad's study and was also seen as among the most difficult. However, Brush found that students were favorable toward language study in junior high but became more negative in high school.

These findings on students' attitudes toward different school subjects present a challenging pattern to explain. Why do American students like some subjects more than others? Why do students' attitudes change toward certain subjects, becoming more negative with time in the case of math and science and somewhat more positive in the case of English? Is the field's difficulty (perceived or actual) the main determinant of students' attitudes? Do student opinions reflect the conditions under which they study different subjects, the nature of the subjects themselves, their degree of success in learning, or some combination of these and other factors?

Brush (1980) tried to explain her findings with regard to English. High school students like English more, believe it is somewhat easier, and feel less anxious in class than they did in junior high. Brush attributes the change to less evaluative classes that allow more student opinion, as when literature is studied. In the earlier grades, when English is more disliked and perceived as more difficult, Brush claims, the curriculum emphasizes grammar, punctuation, spelling, and other topics that have "right answers."

If her argument generalizes to other fields, areas of study that require one correct response or do not use students' own ideas may be liked less by students, and they may also be thought more difficult. Brush assumes that difficulty and dislike are linked. The data we have reviewed are generally consistent with this speculation, but they are not entirely satisfactory. In the case of social studies, for example, students do not like the subject very much but find it rather easy. Social studies courses are often very factual, with emphasis on memorization of specific information and correct answers, but they also contain lessons that use student opinion and experience. Perhaps a more powerful explanation of student attitude patterns would use knowledge of instructional conditions in different areas of study, considered in light of the particular curricular objectives.

Math teachers tend to limit the number of ways that students can access the material, primarily algorithms, that they need to master. These access paths tend to call on specific aptitudes, on which performance largely depends. If only a few ways to learn are available, then students who have different—unutilized—strengths may reasonably infer the field is difficult, feel themselves incompetent, and may come to dislike the subject. We think this is what happens to many students in the years they are learning math in school, and students in science or other fields may be similarly afflicted.

A thorough analysis of instruction in other disciplines would enable us to examine students' access to multiple ways of learning and the nature of program objectives. For example, do science and foreign-language classes operate with a restricted or more flexible set of avenues for student attainment? What range of intellectual objectives is part of instructional programs in these fields? What are the correlates of negative attitudes toward social studies? Most students do not see social studies as difficult and they are not anxious about learning it, but they do not like it. Under what circumstances is that pattern most likely to occur? Does it apply equally to students in group-work and teacher-centered classes?

To be sure, student attitudes do not develop solely in response to instructional approaches. Cultural and family beliefs also play a role (Stigler et al. 1982), as does the actual performance of a given student in the subject. The perceived relevance and importance of a field of study may also influence students' responses, but available data suggest that students' views of the importance of a field are not correlated with their other attitudes. For example, students consistently rate math as a very important area at all school levels, even though many develop negative attitudes toward it (Goodlad 1984; Carpenter et al. 1981). Social studies presents a different pattern, not as easily understood. Goodlad (1984) finds that students assign decreasing importance to social studies over the school grades. At the same time, students rather consistently dislike social studies, although they do not think it is difficult. Perhaps the subject area is perceived as lacking relevance, but detailed enough information is not available. It may also be that a lack of definition of the school subject itself may contribute to this somewhat puzzling pattern of response.

Available data can only be used to suggest relationships between student attitudes and instructional conditions. We do not yet have adequate research to go beyond empirically grounded speculations to empirically grounded conclusions. To investigate these issues, the same students should be studied over time in different classroom settings. Reliable knowledge of their school experiences and assessments of their attitudes, conceptions of what it means to learn in different fields, and school achievement would all be required.

Linking specific attitudes to well-defined curricular programs would be a useful research program. Students who go through different educational programs should develop dissimilar ideas about the meaning of learning, and their attitudes toward a given subject might also diverge. For example, one could compare students in traditional math classes with those in individualized math programs. Do students in individualized programs have different perceptions of mathematics and themselves as learners of math than students in traditional programs? How would students in these programs describe the nature of mathematical knowledge? Do students in individualized programs develop more autonomy in learning, or do they also experience limitations in their quest for mastery?

What consequences arise from different social studies programs? Do children with experience in peer work groups develop skills in interpersonal problem solving, and do the skills transfer to other situations? What attitudes toward cooperation and competition are found in students in group-work programs and students in traditional programs? Slavin (1980, 1983) has shown that increased interpersonal attraction and positive attitudes occur under certain experimental group-work arrangements. Are these consequences of group work in social studies classes as well? Do students studying different content areas in social studies have different attitudes?

Our description of patterns of classroom activity, together with other research on student attitudes and perceptions, leads to a series of questions about the possible impact of instructional experiences on students. The meaning of learning—what students (and teachers) think learning is all about in a given field—is a particularly salient topic for further inquiry.[3] Long after we have forgotten specific facts, algorithms, or concepts taught us in school, we will still hold beliefs about learning different subjects. Those beliefs and attitudes may well condition whether we choose to learn more, how we go about future learning, and what we transmit to our own children. Classroom activity provides routes to learning and develops and reinforces belief systems. Such long-enduring consequences of the school years deserve energetic investigation.

IMPLICATIONS AND REFLECTIONS

The Existential Fallacy and Educational Research

In a study of social phenomena from which recommendations for action or policy may be made, it is important to avoid the existential fallacy, the assumption that knowledge of *what is* tells us *what ought to be*. It is easy to commit the fallacy. Reality as we see it, study it, and live it has a compelling quality, often making it seem that things are the only way they can be. The existential fallacy goes one step further and sees things as they are as morally imperative: if things were "meant" to be otherwise, they would be.[4]

In social science research, particularly educational research, one often encounters a somewhat milder form of the fallacy. Few researchers or writers traffic in moral imperatives or even argue that things ought to be as they are. In fact, much educational writing is directed toward the reverse: things ought to be different in schools and classrooms. Yet the fallacy pervades much research because we do in fact study things as they are and draw conclusions about empirical relationships from things as they are. The danger lies in not recognizing that the arena of school practice that we study is limited. A variety of well-known researchers in education, particularly in the study of teaching (e.g., Gage 1978; Evertson and Green 1986) argue for a strategy that starts with correlational studies of teaching variables and outcomes, and moves to experimental studies. They suggest that a "science" of teaching will be achieved if we discover the variables that relate to desired outcomes in naturally occurring classroom settings. The next step, then, is to induce these behaviors through experimental manipulations and demonstrate their efficacy. While the strategy has some merit, our concern is that it embodies the existential fallacy. The strategy assumes that it is sound to use schools as they are to find principles of effective teaching. A problem arises because schools as they are form a limited subset of all schools as they could feasibly be. If we define effective teaching while limiting ourselves to present-day arrangements, we exclude many possibilities.

The limitations become clear if we consider the matter from a historical point of view. When whole-class recitations and lectures were essentially the only instructional forms used, studies could only identify features of more effective lecturers and recitation leaders. Individualization of instruction through materials and small-group teaching could not have been discovered as effective strategies because they were not in use in the classrooms of the day. Individualized methods are now accepted as valuable, but their adoption and use derived from considerations beyond extant good practice.

For purposes of description, we must study schools as they are.

We expect educational research to contribute to understanding schools as they now function and to help explain why they are as they are. This is all to the good. But if one wants to go beyond description to either theory building or policy, it becomes imperative to reflect about alternatives to present practices. And other considerations, such as values, philosophy, and beliefs about the art of educational practice, enter into thinking about educational alternatives.

There are many ways in which the limits of empirical work must be considered when one moves from description to general theoretical propositions or to policy. The limitations inherent in measurements, samples, and situations must be acknowledged. For example, achievement tests are often used as a pivotal index of schooling effectiveness. A careful assessment of the test content and goals is necessary to decide how broad an inference should be drawn about school learning from the data. This is an example of how we can learn from empirical data only by carefully examining the actual empirical processes used. Similarly, in our study, the meaning of our measurement of involvement must be scrutinized.

The methods used to gather and summarize the empirical data of this study have been described in detail. The reader should be able to judge the validity of our descriptive inferences. When we discuss implications and educational alternatives in the next section, we sometimes move beyond the empirical data. This is as we believe it should be.

Implications

A major finding of this research is that individual teachers vary instructional arrangements as a function of the subject they teach. The mathematics and social studies lessons of almost every teacher we observed had many distinct features. We simply found no correlation in average student involvement in math classes and social studies classes taught by the same teachers to the same students. Teachers do not arrange instructional environments that consistently produce highly involved or less involved children. Elementary school teachers have a more diverse repertoire of teaching behaviors than is often assumed.

Teachers do not have one style of teaching. They use various instructional formats and diverse materials. Teachers expect students to achieve a variety of cognitive goals. Subject matter is the primary, though not exclusive, determinant of alterations in the way teachers teach. In light of our results, the assumption that teachers are very consistent in their methods of instruction must be questioned.

A primary implication of these findings is that teachers can choose educational arrangements from their repertoire. They can maintain and expand the diversity of educational methods they use in the school day through greater awareness of their own teaching choices. To achieve more flexibility, instructional formats and goals that are presently tied to specific subject matters need to be tried in other contexts. Through experimentation, individual teachers should determine how and where the activity settings they already know how to create can be used more effectively. Of course, they should also be open to trying new instructional approaches.

Teacher educators also need to recognize that teachers possess more diverse teaching skills and behaviors than is ordinarily assumed. More reflection needs to be given the adoption of a given activity structure for a particular purpose. Teachers and teacher educators might ask, What are our assumptions about the way to teach reading, math, social studies, and science? Why do we hold these assumptions, and can they be effectively altered?

Subject specialists who train teachers might also find it enlightening and perhaps liberating to talk with one another about their different pedagogical assumptions. Disciplinary lines seem to insulate those who specialize in the teaching of school subjects as much as they do practitioners of the parent disciplines. Teachers seem to be trained to teach each subject without regard to their skills in other fields of teaching. It might help to alter this usual circumstance.

Teachers and teacher educators must try to sort out the necessary in teaching from the conventional—the habitual from the possible. As an example, the use of face-to-face groups could be examined for its utility as a pedagogical practice (cf. Cohen 1984; Sharan et al. 1980; Stodolsky 1984a). There seems no doubt that many teachers find the deployment and management of multiple segments, like small groups, very difficult. In the classes we observed the approach seemed most successful when a curriculum planned for use with small groups had been adopted. In these cases tasks were explicitly designed to be accomplished by small groups of children.

Questions such as the following might be asked to examine the potential of peer work groups: Under the appropriate circumstances, what goals can actually be achieved by small groups of students? What preparation and what kinds of tasks promote successful small-group work? Can groups be used when individual attainment is a prime objective, or do students' possibly unequal contributions to the group mean that less learning will take place than if each pupil worked individually? Why do I use groups in social studies but not in math; does it make good sense? Who really benefits from small-group work and what, if any, "side effects" are associated with its use?

Similar questions could be formulated about other practices and goals that teachers may confine to a particular part of the school curriculum. Another example, not to be elaborated in so much detail, is provision of research experience to students in social studies but not in math. Are there ways in which research skills could be effectively developed and applied in math to meet desired goals? What resources, if any, are available for such research purposes in math? What are the consequences of empowering students to find things out in math and other subjects?

It is often suggested that teachers visit other teachers' classrooms to be exposed to new practices and ideas. We suggest that teachers "visit" with themselves in different teaching contexts. Teachers have the skills and abilities to create different classroom activity structures. They should experiment with untying particular behaviors from their usual context to see if in so doing they might gain flexibility and effectiveness.

Another important implication of our findings is in the area of teacher evaluation. (For an extended discussion of this topic see Stodolsky 1984b.) Elementary school teachers are often evaluated by direct observation. Evaluations that are summative, that entail decisions about retention or promotion, draw on observations. Formative evaluations, in which the purpose is to make suggestions for improvement of teaching, often include observations too.

Current evaluation practice usually involves one or two short observations of a teacher, made without regard to the subject being taught. Our data show that teachers' behavior varies systematically with subject matter and lesson format. To be accurate and fair, observations of a teacher would have to be extensive. Current evaluation procedures assume that all samples of teaching behavior are roughly equivalent, an assumption strongly contradicted by our data. Particularly when employment decisions are to be made, the generalizability of one or two short observations of teachers must be scrutinized. To be sure, observations of teaching can be very useful as one component of an evaluation procedure, particularly a formative one. But an observation of a teacher is an occasion for discussion and reflection about pedagogy, not a datum representative of the individual's teaching skills.

If observations are to be used to formulate a generalizable portrait of a given elementary school teacher, they should include systematic sampling of the variety of subjects taught. Activity segment variables, such as instructional format, should also be considered in developing valid sampling plans for observations of teachers.

The implications of the patterns in our data on student involvement should also be considered. In our study, two activity-setting conditions were associated with higher levels of student involvement in both math and social studies. A highly regular linear pattern was found between increasing cognitive complexity and increases in the level of student involvement. Across pacing conditions, children were most involved when working together. Students also were efficient in their responses to the information contained in segments.

Our finding that children respond positively to cognitive challenge and to the opportunity to work with one another on intellectual tasks arose in the context of examining both a basic and an enrichment field as taught in a wide variety of schools. We examined a somewhat broader and different set of classroom experiences than those used in formulating such models as direct instruction. Those models have been derived primarily from data on reading and math classes—both basic skills which are likely to be taught in a teacher-centered manner. As we have demonstrated, practices found in those basic skills areas were likely to be traditional in format and directed primarily toward lower-mental-process goals.

Our findings point in a very different direction than that adopted by proponents of direct instruction and policy makers of similar persuasion. Our data must stand as a challenge to direct-instruction advocates whose formulation of effective schooling endorses low-level instruction, doled out in small pieces under teacher supervision. At the least their data base is too limited in its subject matter coverage, apart from the serious difficulties with making direct recommendations for practice from correlational data, as described in the section on the existential fallacy.

Teaching intellectually complex skills hardly seems to need justification. Here the nature of the subject matter seems to play a particularly central role. Teachers themselves need to better understand problem solving and application in mathematics, for instance, before they will be comfortable assigning such topics to students. More development of teachers' questioning skills is also needed.

Consideration must also be given to the quality of life for both students and teachers during school. Perhaps our school arrangements are overly determined by the future goals we want to achieve. At times, present arrangements may be legitimated by their future utility though not considered desirable in their own right. The ongoing experiences of all people in schools should concern us. Positive student response to cognitive challenge and complexity, and to the chance to work with friends and peers indicates some of the activities children themselves find engaging. While involvement is not a sufficient way to judge a good school experience, children's reactions and perceptions of school in the here and now deserve more prominence in our deliberations about school settings.

We saw some wonderful and exciting learning situations in the course of our observations. Students were thinking about new ideas, teachers effectively aided students and introduced them to curricular content, students worked alone on interesting or helpful assignments, and they also worked collaboratively in productive ways.

We must concede, however, that our data and those of others show that much activity in elementary schools is mundane and mediocre. We saw busywork, teachers and students making it through the day in desultory fashion, and social and intellectual isolation.

Most of the classes we observed had competent teachers, but most of them seemed to hold a very limited view of what should be learned in school and appeared very skeptical of children's motivation and ability to learn. More often than not, students were treated as receptacles for knowledge that teachers transmit, not active participants in learning. And the nature of the knowledge to be transmitted, often defined by textbooks and other curriculum materials, was chunked so small that its significance was not at all clear.

Many teachers are victims of narrow vision, and they act on that vision with children. Supervisors, publishers, and professors try to "teacher-proof" the educational process and rob teachers of autonomy and professional judgment. In turn, teachers assume children must be made to learn, and so they eliminate choice from the school experience.

Education will not be quickly improved by exhortation or legislation. But we should acknowledge the broader skills and options teachers possess. The flexibility we saw in almost every teacher in our study encourages some optimism. But the flexibility we saw in teachers must be nurtured within schools and wherever teachers learn to teach. Many professional educators want school experiences to be satisfying for children and for themselves. Some of the instructional approaches children found most engaging in the fifth grade might prove liberating for teachers as well. We need to return the world of challenge to teachers while reducing their social and intellectual isolation.

Appendix A
Sample Instruments

Activity Structure Observation Form

Class Code: _____
Observer: _____
Co-observer: _____
Subject Area: _____
   M T W Th F

Date: _____
Number of Adults:
   Teacher(s): _____
   Teacher aide: _____
   Student teacher: _____
   Other (specify): _____
Number of Students: _____
Number of Boys: _____
Number of Girls: _____
For Office Use Only:
   JAT: _____
   SS: _____
   TF: _____
   FK: _____
   DM: _____
   OBS: _____

Information on Blackboard(s):

Miscellaneous Comments:

Activity Structure Observation Form, *Page 2*

A—activity SA—simul. act SWP—sweep Time/Code	pg #; lesson # area/focus in math, SS, etc. Content & Instructional Format	Describe Adults' Activity and Location	Prescribed Material Resources	Additional Resources Used by Teacher
		Location:		
		Location:		

Activity Structure Observation Form, *Page 3*

N & Location of Students	Students' Activities during Task	Specify Options for Students / Specify Any S Input into Options/Structure of Activity
N		
N		

Individual Student Observation Form

Time	Student	On	Off	?	Code	Description of Activities, Materials, Etc.	Location/Group/Group Size

Appendix B
Coding Definitions and Examples

Each code is defined, and examples of segments are provided. If a category applies to only one subject, it is marked (M) for mathematics or (SS) for social studies. Examples are identified with segment ID number preceded by M or SS and follow code definitions. The segment ID number allows identification of the district and classroom observed in our original data files.

INSTRUCTIONAL FORMAT

Instructional format is a global description of the overall action pattern in the segment. The codes are familiar labels for instructional arrangements.

Seatwork. The pupils are working at their desks or other locations on an assignment such as solving math problems in the textbook, workbook, or worksheet. In social studies, children might read the textbook silently and answer related questions in writing. All children have the same task assigned to them.

> In the description of student behavior codes, M211350 and SS031206 are examples.

Diverse Seatwork. The children are working at their desks or other locations on a number of different tasks. Often, they are following an ordered list of tasks or choose among options after completion of a required task. This category applies to a work period or study hall situation. However, if there are subgroups working on a small number of assigned tasks, and they can be clearly identified, segmentation according to tasks is used, and the instructional format is coded as seatwork for each task group.

> In the description of feedback codes, SS072205 and M061109 are examples of diverse seatwork.

Individualized Seatwork (M). The children are at their desks or other locations working on tasks that have been assigned to them or chosen by

142

them on an individual basis. Individualized programs, defined by the criteria below, were in use when this code was applied. Criteria for individualized programs:

(*a*)   Specified learning goals.

(*b*)   Proceeding at individual learning rates.

(*c*)   Instructional placement based on diagnostic testing.

(*d*)   Diagnostically monitored student advancement and provisions for remediation.

Individualized programs may make heavy use of materials, often from a commercially prepared package that includes texts, worksheets, tests, and some audiovisual materials. Some districts prepared their own materials for individualized instruction. In the most elaborate case children had multiple sources they could use for specific instructional needs, allowing the child some options in choosing materials.

M081313 under coding for feedback is an example.

Recitation.   A recitation involves relatively short exchanges between the teacher and students. The teacher is calling on individual children to answer questions or read in turn. The children may be asked to work problems on the board during a recitation segment. Filmstrips that students take turns reading are coded recitation.

M041330 and SS211212 in the codes for student behavior are examples.

Discussion (SS).   Discussions are similar to recitations except that there is usually more exchange between persons in discussions. The teacher leads discussions and often wants to build to some idea or tries to elicit opinions and ideas—not just "right" answers—from students.

Segment: SS031422   Format: Discussion
In this activity segment the teacher wants to develop the concepts of "independence" and "authority." The children have been asked to clear off their desks. The teacher starts out by writing the two terms on the chalkboard and then developing the concept of independence followed by the concept of authority. She asks only open-ended questions; more specifically, she asks about the meaning of these words and for examples to clarify answers. The students volunteer with answers, all of which the teacher writes on the chalkboard, sometimes changing the wording slightly. She does not make any judgmental comments. Exchanges take place only between teacher and students. Students only speak when called upon.

Lecture.   The teacher talks to students at some length about concepts, or the types of problems they are working on. There may be an occasional student question, but the teacher is talking most of the time, imparting information, ideas, and/or skills. This code also applies when the teacher reads out loud.

M031320 described in the section for feedback coding is an illustration.

Segment: SS081415   Format: Lecture
The class watches a filmstrip, "The Life and Times of Abraham Lincoln." Students take turns reading aloud the passages on the filmstrip. After short intervals, the teacher turns off the projector to elaborate on the lifestyle and society of Lincoln's time and compare them with today's. He extensively explicates differences and similarities between then and now and tries to relate his comparison to learning experiences the children have had. He also asks some questions, but they are mostly of a factual nature—defining terms, etc.

Demonstration.   The teacher shows how to do an experiment, how to solve a problem, or how to make something.

SS081422 in the coding for cognitive level is an example.

Segment: M072103   Format: Demonstration
The teacher has handed out three commercially prepared worksheets to be completed at home. She stands in front of the class and explains the third one, entitled "Graphing Pictures." The worksheet has three grids and three sets of ordered number pairs which result in a picture when graphed correctly. The teacher mentions the similarity between graphing number pairs and stock values. She explains the function of the first and second number in the ordered pair and demonstrates the actual plotting. She shows how to find the value of the first number by going across the grid, finding the value of the second number by going up in the coordinate system. The children are working on the first graph and are encouraged to help each other. After a few number pairs are plotted, the teacher leads the class to the next two graphs and demonstrates an example. Again, she points out that X-values are to be looked up first in the grid horizontally, followed by the vertical Y-values.

Checking Work.   The pupils correct their homework, seatwork, or tests. Usually, the teacher provides short answers or has the children take turns in reading them off. This instructional format is an "efficient," fairly short one. It does not include instructional explanations or additional teacher or student questions of a substantive nature. Often, scores or the number of right answers are reported orally to the teacher at the end of the segment.

Segment M021107 described in the coding for cognitive level is an illustration.

Segment: SS021207   Format: Checking Work
The class is correcting previous assignments in a workbook. The teacher proceeds page by page, reading aloud the number of each question and the letter of the correct answer, which belongs to a list of answers at the bottom of the page. A few times, students interrupt to present a different answer which they believe to be correct. If reasonable, objections to the prescribed answers are accepted by the teacher. At the end, students count the number of right and wrong answers and figure out their percentage for grading purposes. Calling out percentages of right and wrong answers, the teacher has the students raise hands. Then the workbooks are collected.

Test/quiz.   The children are taking a test or quiz, written or orally administered.

   Two descriptions of this format code, M021118 and SS061205, are in the section describing codes for feedback.

Group Work.   The children are divided into groups, with at least two children working together. Each group works on a joint task—that is, children are sharing a common activity that requires interdependent actions. Tasks may be similar or different across groups. Each group constitutes a separate segment—thus, several group-work segments usually exist simultaneously.

   SS081207 in the codes for cognitive level is an illustration. Group work rarely occurred in mathematics.

Film Audiovisual (SS).   The children are watching and/or listening to films, tapes, etc. This code does not apply if discussion or recitation is frequently interspersed.

   SS211221 in the description of the student behavior codes is an example. The code was not used for any of the mathematics segments since tapes were only used in individualized programs and the code for individualized seatwork as the format took precedence.

Contests, Learning Games.   The instructional activities include cognitive games or contests that may involve all or part of the class.

   Examples are provided in the descriptions of coding for student behavior (M081106) and the coding for feedback (SS051208).

Student Reports (SS).   One or more students share information, talk or read to the class. Book chats, current events, or group reports are common examples.

An illustration is given in the description of coding for feedback (SS072218). This code did not apply to any mathematics segment.

Giving Instructions.   The teacher is telling the children the plan for an activity or time period, what to do when, what kinds of materials to use, etc. The teacher may briefly go over rules, give homework assignments or seatwork assignments, and issue reminders. Giving instructions may relate to the task at hand, but it is basically procedural and not substantive.

SS011202 in the section on coding student behavior and M063115 in the section on coding feedback illustrate this format.

Task Preparation.   Task preparation is more than a brief reminder of how to do a task (as is found in Giving Instructions). The teacher is substantively preparing the students for upcoming tasks. He or she may read instructions to them and illustrate a few problems. This format is almost always followed by a seatwork or group-work segment.

An example of a social studies segment (SS081202) is provided in the description of coding for cognitive level.

Segment: M063114   Format: Task Preparation
After the class has finished correcting homework, the teacher prepares the children for the upcoming assignment. She moves to the chalkboard and works out one example of the problems on the next page in the text. Then she announces the next two pages as the assignment for the following two days and asks the students to start working. The preparation takes only three minutes. During this time the students listen and quietly watch the teacher.

Tutoring (M).   A teacher, another adult, or a child is teaching another child.

M021127 described in the feedback section is an example.

Stock Market (SS).   This instructional format was created to enable coding of activity segments observed in only one classroom. The activity included keeping daily records of stock prices in the form of a graph. In these segments the teacher read off current market values of stocks and each child plotted the value of his or her stock on graph paper. Occasionally economic trends were discussed. The activity integrated both subject matters—social studies and mathematics—but was considered social studies because of the emphasis on economics.

SS072406 in the section on feedback coding is an example.

Transition/Organizing. The children are moving from one activity to another, one place to another; are getting things ready, or putting them away. During a transition most children are not attending to an academic learning task. Segments coded "transition" do not display any instructional quality and therefore are excluded from descriptive and quantitative analysis of instructional activity segments.

PACING

The term *pacing* is borrowed from Gump (1967). It refers to who is determining the rate of work in an activity segment. The variable has also been used by Grannis (1978) and called *press*. Four categories of pacing were identified and coded.

Teacher Pacing. The child works or attends at a rate set by the teacher, not by his or her own desires. This occurs when the teacher is running a subgroup or whole-class activity—for instance, a recitation, lecture, or demonstration.

M011124 and SS031219 in the coding of cognitive level are examples.

Child Pacing. This code is applied to segments in which the child determines his or her own rate of work, though the teacher may intermittently monitor or interact with students. Instructional situations, such as seatwork, student reports, or reading, are usually child paced.

M041302 and SS211407 in the coding of cognitive level are examples.

Cooperative (Child-Child) Pacing. The children cooperatively control the pace when working together on a joint project or task. This code finds more application in social studies, where group-work projects occur more often— for instance, when children play the simulation game "Sailing to the New World," paint murals of the Old West, or work on a career display. In mathematics, cooperative pacing is found when students are in a tutoring situation or are playing a cognitive game such as "Contig."

SS081215 in cognitive-level coding and M081106 in student behavior codes are examples.

Mechanical Pacing. This code is used for instructional activities in which the work is set by a technical device, commonly an audiovisual aid. When watching a film or listening to a record neither the teacher nor the students control the pace. This code applied only to social studies segments.

SS211221 in student behavior codes is an example.

COGNITIVE LEVEL

Cognitive-level codes refer to the educational objectives or intellectual goals of instructional tasks and activities as they can be inferred from observations of classroom lessons. Although social and affective goals are also desired in schools, we have not systematically coded them. Since educational objectives are not always achieved, we coded both the expected cognitive level and the actual cognitive level. Ordinarily these are the same, but occasionally the desired cognitive process will not be achieved or, conversely, students will go beyond task demands to a more cognitively complex performance.

We coded the main cognitive level or process in each segment. We adapted the broad categories of the *Taxonomy of Educational Objectives* (Bloom et al. 1956) and categories suggested by Orlandi (1971) in his discussion of social studies programs.

The coding of cognitive level and process is partially hierarchical in the same sense that the *Taxonomy* follows a hierarchy built on complexity. In addition there are some categories that cross a number of taxonomic levels but represent sets of cognitive processes and skills important in social studies.

Receiving and Recalling Information/Facts (Level One). This lower-mental-process category is essentially identical to the Knowledge level in the *Taxonomy.* In segments coded at this level, students receive information (or facts) through lecture, demonstrations, student reports, tapes and/or reading. Recall and recognition are often demanded in seatwork tasks, in texts, and in recitations in which children answer teacher-posed questions.

Segment M011124   Format: Lecture
The teacher has divided the class into three seatwork groups and is lecturing a group of eight children about parts of fractions. This topic is the subject of the textbook problems assigned to the students. The teacher reminds the students of a definition of a fraction.

Segment M021107   Format: Checking Work
Students exchange math papers for grading while the teacher quickly writes the answers to the twelve problems on the blackboard. The problems involve multiplication of fractions. Students check and return their papers. The teacher then reads off the number of each problem and asks students to raise their hands if they missed the problem. This procedure is conducted quickly and with no substantive discussion of the problem.

Segment SS031219   Format: Recitation
The teacher leads the whole class in a recitation using the social studies text and map skills workbook. His rapid-fire questions directed at individual students emphasize review of the textbook material on the American

colonies—e.g., "How many colonies were there?" "What is the House of Lords?" and recall of geographical terms presented in the map workbook— e.g., "What is the equator?" "What is a diameter?"

Segment SS081202   Format: Task Preparation
Students are seated at their desks looking over rule sheets for a simulation game being used for the social studies unit on the settlement of the American colonies. The teacher goes over the instructions, calling on students to state the rules for recording game points and asking them to read certain sections of the rule sheets.

Concepts and Skills (Level Two).   At this level children learn basic ideas in a subject going beyond isolated facts to concepts and patterns of facts and ideas. Comprehension, including the ability to restate information, and classification of information is coded at this level. Learning arithmetic algorithms and practicing them is a major component of cognitive processes coded here.

At Level Two, students are not only exposed to information, but the emphasis is on teaching and learning concepts and skills. In mathematics, concepts and computational algorithms, such as manipulations with fractions and decimals, are introduced, and students practice these skills. In social studies, students may summarize a paragraph in their own words or restate an idea from written materials; they may also classify, compare, and contrast information.

When children work together in groups, it is especially important to assess the actual and expected cognitive processes. Decision making within a group, if it is based on comparing and contrasting alternatives without considerable cognitive depth, is coded at Level Two for the actual cognitive level of the segment. This may occur even though the expected cognitive level is more complex.

Segment M041302   Format: Seatwork
The whole class is engaged in individual seatwork which involves completing a set of problems in the math textbook. The problems are short-answer, and require students to practice their skills in identifying correct fractional terms (for pictures of shaded figures and written statements) and adding simple fractions. The teacher circulates and answers a few student questions.

Segment SS041211   Format: Recitation
The teacher is leading a recitation with the whole class about "goods and services" as the students follow along in their workbooks. The teacher reads a series of questions from her teacher's manual about this topic—e.g., "What does a baker supply? What does a minister? A good or a service?" Students write the answer in their workbooks after each response. She then discusses the difference between goods and services and asks the class, "Can anyone give a definition of goods and services in their own words?"

One student answers her question. The teacher proceeds to ask the class to look up *goods* and *services* in their dictionaries, and one student reads the definitions aloud from the dictionary.

Categories three and four address research skills, a major objective in social studies. They are not completely hierarchical in the sense of being more cognitively complex than the preceding levels. They are important cognitive components of some social studies instructional programs.

Research Skills A: Location of Information (Level Three).   In these segments, students use such reference materials as encyclopedias, atlases, and dictionaries to obtain information, usually for written reports. This cognitive category includes activities that range across both lower and higher mental processes but often center around obtaining and comprehending information as well as actually practicing the reference-tool skills. Thus this category is often similar to Level Two but can be more complex when students are obtaining information from multiple sources.

Segments SS211407, SS211408   Format: Seatwork
In both of these seatwork segments, students are working individually on state reports. Each student has been assigned a state and is expected to write a report using several references. In one of the segments (211407) a group of five students look up information in reference books at the Learning Resource Center. In the other segment (211408) the students research their reports using classroom reference materials—e.g., encyclopedia, almanac, and an opaque map of the states. Some of the students go to the teacher with their questions about the research—e.g., "How do you look up the governor of the state?"

Research Skills B: Use and Interpretation of Symbolic and Graphic Data (Level Four).   Students work with nonverbal symbolic data, reading and acquiring skills to read maps, graphs, charts, tables, and cartoons. Students make maps, graph data, and create charts to display information. Segments coded in this category include a number of other cognitive levels but are at least Level Two.

Segment SS081420   Format: Contest
The whole class is involved in a contest activity called "Game of the Fifty States." The teacher divides the class into two teams with captains, and a member of each team comes up to the front of the room. Then, the teacher holds up a flash card with the outline of a state, and the first team member to recognize it wins a point for his or her team. The tempo is fast-paced.

Segment SS081422   Format: Demonstration
The teacher lectures to the whole class about how a Mercator projection distorts the poles. He instructs the students to roll their soft-cover atlases so as to illustrate the difference between the shape of a rolled map and a

globe. The class proceeds to turn to the maps in their atlases—following along as the teacher reviews certain geographic locations.

Application of Concepts and Skills (Level Five). This is a higher-mental-process activity. Concepts and skills are applied to new but familiar situations. In mathematics, for example, a student who is asked to solve a story or word problem must decide which computational procedure to use and then apply it. Social studies activities coded here involve transferring ideas from one context to another—for example, applying the concept of ecological niche to a new cultural setting, or using methods of conflict resolution to solve a hypothetical interpersonal problem. Role-playing activities are usually coded here as well. In a group problem-solving situation, the actual cognitive level would be coded "Application" if decision making in the group follows a substantive discussion but lacks evaluative quality.

Segment M062107   Format: Recitation
The teacher is standing at the blackboard leading a recitation for one math group (approximately half the class), while the other students sit quietly at their desks. She asks students in the math group to turn to a page in their math texts and proceeds to review the math problems there. These problems will be assigned as seatwork in the next segment. The problems require students to translate a story problem into an equation—e.g., "Mary had a certain number of dollars. She spent such and such. How much did she have left?" After a student reads a problem from the text, the teacher elaborates by asking questions like, "What kind of problem is that?" "What kind of equation will we do with that?" and goes on to illustrate a solution on the blackboard.

Segment SS081215   Format: Group Work
Six students are working at their desks on a problem that is part of the social studies simulation game "Sailing to the New World." Using calculators and worksheets, they complete a set of computations for ordering their supplies for sailing to America. The activity is complicated by the fact that supplies have different weights and the group is restricted to a certain weight. This group works carefully, sorting their supply cards into three equal piles and double-checking their calculations.

Higher Mental Processes (Level Six). All other higher processes in the *Taxonomy* beyond "Application" are included in this code. At the fifth-grade level, these processes do not occur frequently, and therefore separate categories did not seem warranted. This category includes production of generalizations and hypotheses, as well as the processes of analysis, synthesis, and evaluation described in the *Taxonomy*. The solution of an unfamiliar problem in mathematics would be coded here, as would generating a method of solution or devising a rule for a variety of problems. However, we found only one math segment at this level in all of our observations.

In social studies, students may state hypotheses or make generalizations when comparing cultures or historical and social events. The level of synthesis might be reached when students write a report using more than one reference source. Decision making of groups or individuals that displays awareness and consideration of alternatives using reasoning and evaluation is coded here.

Segment SS081207   Format: Group Work
A group of five students are discussing the merits of three alternative reasons for sailing to the New World. This activity is part of a simulation game used for the social studies unit on the settlement of the American colonies. The teacher has identified in her preparation that there are certain consequences for each decision—e.g., "If you are sent by the government you pay half of your land to the government"—and reminds the students that these should be considered when making the final decision. The task requires students to make one group decision, and the students in this segment discuss their options seriously. In addition, they talk about how to arrive at the decision, whether to vote or draw lots, etc.

Segments SS091271-091278   Format: Group Work
Groups of two and three students are spread around the room playing rounds of "The Crossing Place Hunting Game," which is part of the *MACOS* curriculum unit on Eskimos. The game requires players to apply different strategies in a mock hunt of caribou. A game board and die are used to play the game. In her instructions, the teacher tells the students to "talk about a strategy that will help you kill more caribou on the next game." After completing three rounds, students fill out a worksheet with questions dealing with analysis and synthesis of their game strategies—e.g., "How is this game similar to a real caribou hunt at a crossing place?" "What advantages does the crossing place method have over the bow and arrow method?"

Not Cognitive.   This category was used for segments in which the cognitive content seemed minimal or not relevant. Sometimes these segments were oriented toward other primary goals: nurturing creativity or social or affective outcomes. In a number of instances, children produced murals or made craft projects. In these cases it seemed that the tasks had little cognitive demand after the planning phases. We do not mean to imply that artistic work is not cognitive, but the particular quality of the segments involved did not suggest cognitive learning or skill, often because the tasks were too easy or projects extended too long.

Segments SS071202   Format: Diverse Seatwork
Students are working in a diverse seatwork situation, pursuing a variety of
craft activities—e.g., finger knitting, making posters, or sewing in
preparation for a classroom open house. While the purpose of these
activities is to construct crafts representative of Israel, this focus is lost in
the actual process of designing and making the projects. Several students
wander or stand around the room during these segments. This activity
continues over seven nonconsecutive instructional days.

STUDENT BEHAVIOR

The code for student behavior describes the students' activities during the
instructional segment. We coded twenty-eight categories. About a third of
the categories are subject specific: eight are descriptive of student behavior
in social studies lessons only (S), while two more describe student activities
used only in mathematics (M). The remaining categories for student
behavior could be applied to both mathematics and social studies instruction
but often occurred more often in one of the subjects. Examples are not
provided if the activity pattern is very apparent.

Question/Answer.   The students are asking questions and/or giving
answers orally. This code describes the typical student behavior during
recitations.

Segment: M041330   Format: Recitation
The topic of this recitation is cancelling when multiplying fractions. The
teacher puts five examples on the chalkboard and leads the class through
them step by step. At each step the students provide answers to the
teacher's inquiry about what to do next and why. They seem to be highly
attentive throughout this exercise.

Segment: SS211212   Format: Recitation
This recitation is based on a previous assignment about types of jobs that
children found in the classified ad section of local newspapers. They report
on some of the jobs listed and answer additional questions put by the teacher
for clarification. Typical questions are, "What type of education do you need
for this job?" "What is the income?" "Is it a day or night job?" "Does the job
require standing or sitting?" The child reporting and others volunteer to
answer these questions.

Read/Oral.   One or more students are reading orally from a textbook,
magazine or other similar source as other pupils listen.

Solve/Desk.   Students are solving problems either mentally or on paper at
their desks. They may be working on a series of mathematics problems or

on short-answer questions in social studies. Essay-type answers are not coded here but in the category "Write."

Segment: M211350   Format: Seatwork
A previous recitation session had served to acquaint the children with the task requirements of the seatwork. The task is to add mixed numbers with like denominators. Two of the problems in the text are story problems similar to the ones solved in the recitation session. The children work quietly at their desks. Feedback is provided largely by the textbook.

Segment: SS031206   Format: Seatwork
The children are assigned a mimeographed worksheet to complete at their desks. They define terms used in social studies or in language arts such as *noun, longitude, Cortez, median,* with the help of their social studies and language arts textbooks and dictionaries. The teacher is also available to answer questions.

Blackboard/Solve.   One or more students are solving problems at the blackboard while the remainder of the class solve the same problems on paper at their desks.

Segment: M021320   Format: Contest
In this skill contest on multiplication of fractions the six rows in this classroom represent six teams competing against each other. A different student from each row comes up to the chalkboard to solve a problem as quickly and accurately as possible at each turn. The problem is to be solved by all students in class. However, only competitors at the board gain points for their team. The first student with the correct solution gains two more points than the second one, while the last student earns no points.

Blackboard/Watch.   One or more students are solving problems at the blackboard while the remainder of the class passively watches from their desks.

Segment: M011102   Format: Recitation
The class is divided into three groups according to achievement. In this segment the teacher works with nine students on adding fractions with unlike denominators. She solves three examples at the chalkboard asking the students how to proceed next at each step. Then, she puts seven different problems on the board and asks seven students to solve them on the board. The students at the board take turns explaining the steps involved to obtain the answer to their problem, while the others watch. Finally, the two students who have not been at the board previously get their turn and explain two additional problems to the group.

AV/Recitation (SS).   The students are watching a filmstrip and take turns reading the accompanying text out loud. The teacher makes comments and intersperses questions.

Choral (M).   The students respond in unison to the teacher's questions.

Checking Work.   The students are correcting homework, seatwork, or tests as the teacher or some of the students read off answers or write answers on the blackboard. There is no recitation involved; no explanations are given—only the correct answers for the assignment are provided.

Segment M021107 in the section on cognitive level is an example.

Discuss/Listen.   The students are engaged in a discussion, or they may be listening to a discussion taking place. The discussion may engage the teacher and the whole class, the teacher and a subset of the class, or members of a cooperative group.

SS081207 in the section on cognitive level is an example.

Film/AV (SS).   The students are watching a film or are listening to a record or tape. This code includes watching a filmstrip accompanied by a record.

Segment: SS211221   Format: Film/AV
The students quietly watch a filmstrip about life and culture in the thirteen colonies. The teacher does not comment throughout the six-minute showing. The students are very attentive. They enthusiastically clap when the filmstrip ends.

Listening.   The students passively listen to and watch the teacher. They may have occasional questions, but the teacher does most of the talking and is the center of attention. This code also applies when students are listening to one or more peers giving a report.

Segment: SS011202   Format: Giving Instructions
The teacher explains a new class project for about eight minutes to a group of students. The group is to choose an aspect of black history and clip related stories and pictures out of magazines and newspapers. Then students have to write a report accompanying the materials, which will be collected in book form. Today's task is to select a worthwhile topic of research. While the project is explained, the students sit at their desks and listen.

Read/Silent.   The students are reading silently at their desks. Materials may include either task- or subject-related reading or non-task-related materials such as fiction books or magazines.

Test.   The students are taking a test or quiz which is either written or orally administered.

Write (SS).   The students may copy questions from the textbook or blackboard and/or answer questions in essay form. They may write a composition.

Segment: SS091438   Format: Group Work
Three students work cooperatively on two printed worksheets. The cognitively demanding task requires the students to synthesize information from several sources to adequately answer questions about the Netsilik Eskimos. The students respond in written form.

Research (SS).   The students are engaged in research using textbooks, encyclopedias, and other research materials.

Segment: SS041446   Format: Group Work
In this segment two children cooperate in collecting some necessary information for their career project. The project includes a report about a career, the making of a poster advertising the services of the someone in such a career, and a presentation of the product associated with it. The children use encyclopedias and other available resources from the classroom and the library and make notes.

Drawing/Painting (SS).   The students are drawing or painting posters, murals, and the like.

Maps (SS).   The students are drawing or using maps.

Segment: SS031214   Format: Seatwork
After a very brief recitation session which served as an introduction to basic map skills, the students are to complete a workbook assignment on map skills. Since they are not allowed to write in the workbooks they copy the map with tracing paper and then make further drawings to complete the tasks stated at the bottom of the workbook page.

Graphs.   The students are making or using graphs and/or charts.

Segment SS031403 in the section on feedback is an example.

Crafts.   The students are making crafts items.

Segment: SS071229   Format: Group Work
Students are working in small groups on craft projects under the UNESCO motto "1979, The Year of the Child." The projects in this class focus on the child in Israeli culture. Students prepare posters, weavings, book markers, etc. Three children are sewing with yarn on burlap to create a wall hanging.

Manipulatives.   The students are using manipulatives such as protractors, rulers, and metric sticks.

Tutor (M).   One student is tutoring or instructing another student.

Segment M021127 in the section on feedback is an example.

Game—Cognitive.   The students are playing a subject-related game with one or several partners. The game has a cognitive component. Examples of cognitive games are "Contig" and "Math Bingo" in mathematics, "Caribou Hunt Game" and "In-Out Game" in social studies.

Segment: M081106   Format: Contest
In this segment a group of five students play "Contig" in the math laboratory. One student is the scorekeeper, while the other four play in teams of two against each other. The game requires students to choose an operation such that it will make a true number sentence out of three numbers obtained by throwing dice.

Rehearse Play (SS).   The students are rehearsing for a play.

Contest.   The students are participating in a contest either individually or in teams. An example is a contest using knowledge of state capitals in a two-team competition run like a spelling bee.

Readying/Transition.   The students are getting ready for instruction. This includes putting books away, taking other books or papers out, and waiting for the teacher to start the next instructional activity.

Question/Answer—Oral Reading.   The students are reading orally from a textbook, magazine, etc., and they answer questions that the teacher orally intersperses.

Segment: SS051421   Format: Recitation
In this recitation segment, the teacher calls on one student at a time to read aloud a paragraph in the text. After each paragraph the teacher paraphrases the content in one or two sentences and asks questions suggested by the teachers' manual. Several children supply answers until the teacher obtains the specific one she is looking for. Sometimes she interrupts during the reading to ask questions clarifying definitions of terms.

Other (SS).   The students exhibit behavior not described by any of the above codes.

Variety.   The students exhibit a variety of the behaviors described above in one segment.

TEACHER LEADERSHIP ROLE

The coding for teacher leadership is adapted from Gump (1967). The codes describe the teacher's role and function in the activity segments.

Not in Segment. The teacher is not helping the students in this segment; he or she is not clearly or consistently attending to this activity. The pupils' action is not directed or aided by the teacher. The teacher is usually busy in another segment.

Watcher/Helper—Intermittent. The teacher is watching and helping the students with their assigned tasks. The teacher may circulate, may stand at the back of the room, or may be at the teacher's desk. At times, the students may approach the teacher for help.

Watcher/Helper—Continuous. In this category, the teacher's actions are focused on watching and helping the students with their assigned tasks. The teacher may circulate, paying much attention to the students' progress and needs. From the students' perspective, the teacher would be aware of children needing assistance. Vigilance is not for discipline but for instructional goals. The continuous watcher/helper seems to be a "with-it" teacher.

Recitation Leader. The teacher asks for reciters, comments on answers, and may quiz. He or she may direct a discussion and/or give brief, interspersed explanations.

Instructor. The teacher tells the students how to make something, what some facts are, etc. This is not done in a recitation format; the children are not asked for any contributions. Information is handed out: the teacher gives instructions, lectures, or demonstrates. The teacher may answer some students questions and may also briefly check to see whether they understand the instructions.

Action Director. The teacher gives directions for cleanup, issues orders to manage an activity, leads a song, or sets up team games. Rather than supplying the core action, the teacher becomes the key to the action by demanding that the students do something.

Participator. The teacher is not leading the activity but genuinely participates along with the others. The teacher may sing with, discuss with, or play a game with the children.

Reader. The teacher reads aloud to the children.

Tester. The teacher administers a test or quiz to the children, either reading the questions aloud or proctoring as they work silently.

FEEDBACK

Feedback refers to ways in which students can gain information about the correctness of their performance and/or get assistance in accomplishing a task. By the fifth-grade level, feedback is often delayed; however, this category was applied to feedback sources available to children while a segment was in operation.

The feedback variable was coded for segments under all pacing conditions, but coding varied somewhat depending on the pacing condition. Under child-paced and teacher-paced segments we coded the feedback categories as described below. In cooperatively paced segments we coded feedback categories but made the assumption that student feedback—the availability of children to one another—was always present. Thus in cooperative segments, a category code is actually student feedback *plus* the relevant category.

There are a variety of types of feedback. Feedback associated with materials is one major type. Worksheets with answers, manipulative devices, and textbooks with illustrations are examples of feedback that comes with the materials in use. Another major class of feedback is that provided by other people—teachers or children. Combinations of teacher and material feedback also occur.

There are situations in which feedback does not seem relevant. Such situations were coded "not applicable" for feedback. These were primarily segments in which children were receiving information and in which questions and answers were in no way expected. The most common instances were audiovisual segments such as showing a film, or instruction segments that were highly routinized. Segments in which feedback was coded "none" were distinguished from those coded "not applicable" by the fact that a segment coded "none" might have appropriately contained feedback but did not, whereas the "not applicable" segments did not seem to require feedback.

The codes used for feedback are defined and illustrated below. Combinations of categories are not defined, but all categories and combinations used are listed.
1. None.
2. Manipulatives or Self-Correcting Materials.
3. Books.
4. Self-Check.
5. Student Feedback.
6. Teacher—Low.
7. Teacher—High.

8. Not Applicable.
9. Textbook Only.
10. Teacher—Low and 2, 3, and/or 4.
11. Teacher—Low and Textbook (9).
12. Teacher—High and 2, 3, and/or 4.

None. The children have no way to check on the correctness of their answers or procedures. They are using materials that do not have answers or other feedback properties. They are not given access to the teacher or other children as information sources, or they do not approach the teacher who might be available to help them. A common example of this code occurs when children are taking tests or working on a set of problems on a ditto sheet. If a child is using a textbook, the nature of the task and the text must be considered. If, for example, the task is to answer factual questions in social studies, the answers may be available to help them. A common example of this code occurs when children are taking tests or working on a set of problems on a ditto sheet. If a child is using a textbook the nature of the task and the text must be considered. If, for example, the task is to answer factual questions in social studies, the answers may be available in the text, thus providing a feedback source. In math, if the text does not contain explanations or examples, and no other feedback is available, feedback is coded as "none." In teacher-paced segments, "none" is coded when there is no exchange between students and teachers about correctness or children's understanding of work. For example, in some recitations or lecture segments, the "none" code occurs even though it would have been possible for feedback to occur in the segment. For cooperative segments a code of "none" cannot occur, since it is assumed that children working in a group are available to each other.

Segment: M021118   Format: Test
Students take a short quiz. The teacher had written ten problems on the chalkboard before class and now asks the students to solve them in a ten-minute time period on a sheet of paper. The teacher supervises the class, extends the time for the quiz, but does not assist in problem solving.

Segment: SS072406   Format: Stocks
In this brief segment—it lasts only three minutes—a stock market report based on the previous day is given by the teacher to update the students on their chosen stocks' value. She recites the letters of the alphabet, the children call out names of companies whose names begin with that letter and whose stock they bought. Then she reads the current price, and the children record it on graph paper. The stock graphs have been kept for some time.

Manipulatives or Self-Correcting Materials. Manipulative or self-correcting materials are those in which the materials themselves provide information about correctness through operating with them. Measuring devices, hand calculators, computers, tracing paper, and the like are included here.

These feedback mechanisms are more common in mathematics than in social studies. Some individualized instructional programs use such devices in the course of instruction. For example, children receive instruction by listening to tapes or through computer assistance. Manipulatives can also be seen during math seatwork, when children use hand calculators for computations or protractors and rulers for measuring purposes. In group work situations, children can be found practicing basic arithmetic facts with flashcards or using other manipulatives.

Autotelic devices are rarely used in social studies. Our observers recorded use of flashcards for state names, tracing paper, and calculators in a few instances.

Segment: M081313   Format: Individualized Seatwork
As part of the individualized instruction offered in this classroom, one student receives audio instructions in an AV-equipped room. While listening to the tape, which is part of an SRA learning kit, he fills in his worksheet.

Segment: SS031217   Format: Seatwork
During seatwork the students spend most of their time copying the U.S. map in their *Map Skills Book* using tracing paper. They include each state with its name and even trace the compass rose. After having completed the map, students answer the nine questions on geography at the bottom of the same page.

Books (SS).   The children are using books or other reference materials which have discursive text. Fiction may be included here. Atlases and other map materials are also included as reference materials. Textbooks in regular use are not coded here, but a curriculum set with reference materials might be.

It appears that books other than textbooks are not used in mathematics. (Only one math segment was coded "Books," and here the teacher had told the children that those who had completed the assignment could read fiction.) In social studies this code applied when children tried to locate information for class projects or student reports, often in libraries or resource centers. Children also looked up definitions of new terms in dictionaries or completed map skill exercises with the help of atlases.

Segment: SS072205   Format: Diverse Seatwork
The nine students in this segment use the resources in the library for their upcoming presentations on an ancient civilization of their choice. The teacher is with the rest of the class in their classroom.

Self-check.   The teacher explains how the children can check their own work. This code applies when answer sheets or teachers' manuals are made available for checking. The teacher may explain an algorithm or method for checking work that does not use answer sheets but allows the child to assess correctness. For instance using multiplication to check division would be a self-check algorithm.

This code is more applicable in mathematics than in social studies. Commonly, segments with children using individualized learning packages accompanied by answer sheets fall into this category. Also, seatwork in some traditional classes is arranged so that children go to the teacher's desk to compare their answers with an answer sheet or teacher's manual.

Segment: M041338   Format: Seatwork
In this segment students learn concepts and practice computational skills by solving the assigned problems in their workbook. Though the teacher does talk to one or two of her students, her attention is focused on finding a specific ditto master. As usual, students check their answers by going to the teacher's desk and comparing them with the answer sheets.

Segment: SS211224   Format: Seatwork
The students are working on a photocopy of the U.S. map. They outline the colonies as they were before they changed to states, then they label them and color them in. A map displayed with the overhead projector aids in checking their work. There is hardly any teacher-student interaction.

Student Feedback.   Children give information or feedback to one another. Children check each other's work or give assistance to one another. In mathematics, children most commonly provide feedback to each other when they play learning games or are in a tutoring situation. Working jointly on a written assignment occurs less often. In social studies, the most likely instructional situations with this code are group work and learning games.

This code finds application in cooperative group work only if no other source of feedback is available to the group. If additional sources of feedback are in operation, this code is superseded by the appropriate code for the other feedback source, as student feedback is assumed as well.

Segment: M021127   Format: Tutoring
At the teacher's request, a student who has missed several days of school is taught by another student how to multiply fractions. There is a lot of interaction between the two. While talking, the tutor repeatedly points at examples written on a sheet of paper.

Segment: SS041439   Format: Learning Games
In the previous segment, the teacher introduced rebuses on a commercial worksheet. Now the students make up their own rebuses for names of states, and they present them to the class. One or two students at a time

draw their solution on the chalkboard, and the others try to find the name of the state. Though the teacher participates in solving the puzzle, the feedback is provided by students.

Teacher—Low.   This code requires the teacher to be in the segment and available to the children. She or he provides occasional answers, corrections, and comments to children individually or in groups. The teacher may circulate or stay at some fixed location. The nature of the exchanges between teachers and students must be substantive and have a feedback quality—that is, they are motivated by student behaviors that need correction or reinforcement about the learning process itself. The teacher's comments about deportment and procedure are not considered feedback.

The low category of teacher feedback is applied when the teacher's level of activity is low to moderate in regard to the proportion of time of a segment spent in contact with children and with regard to the number of children contacted. Also a judgment is made about the qualitative depth involved in the responses given to children. In order for this category to be coded, more than one child has to be contacted for feedback purposes. No other sources of feedback can be operating at the same time. If other feedback sources are in the segment, then a combination code should be used.

In segments coded as "Teacher Feedback—Low," children tended to complete assignments on worksheets, gave reports, played instructional games or worked on their group projects with some assistance from the teacher. Many recitations were coded in this category, as was most supervised child-paced work.

Segment: M031109   Format: Seatwork
The teacher hands out worksheets on operations with fractions, to be started in class and finished at home. He indicates that students should ask him for help if they need any. He moves around the room, stops at children's desks, or asks them to come up to him when they raise their hands. His interactions with children are frequent but short. He indicates what is wrong and shows quickly how to do it right, but he does not explain the underlying concept, which is apparently not well understood.

Segment: SS031403   Format: Seatwork
The children are making a chart on notebook paper listing each state and its products as displayed by a map on one of the commercial worksheets produced by the Data Bank System. The teacher walks around, checks the children's progress, and answers short questions. In particular, she helps them clarify how to check the correct spelling of the state names but asks them to use dictionaries and maps only after they have completed the charts. Students who have not finished the assignment at the end of the period are asked to take it home for completion.

Teacher—High. The teacher provides correct answers and makes diagnostic comments to children individually or in groups. This occurs many times throughout the segment. The teacher-student interaction is frequent and substantial. The greater frequency and depth of feedback distinguishes teacher—high from teacher—low.

In many segments coded "Teacher—High" there is a limited use of instructional materials. The code was often used for recitation segments in mathematics with an active teacher applying diagnostic skills to help students understand concepts and algorithms. In social studies the teacher elaborated on answers given during recitation and discussion. Students' answers were expanded, leading to new ideas and questions.

Segment: M031320   Format: Lecture
In this lecture the teacher (1) writes definitions of terms related to fractions accompanied by examples on the chalkboard, and (2) introduces the concept of improper fractions through graphic illustrations on the board. Students are instructed to take notes, and she asks related questions to make sure that they are following her throughout her lecture. She also involves them in the development of the concept of improper fractions by using examples they can relate to and posing questions to test their understanding.

Segment: SS072218   Format: Student Reports
This class spends forty minutes on current events. Students have picked political and social issues featured in newspapers, magazines or on television (e.g., "60 Minutes") and report on them in class. Some of the topics are the peace treaty between Israel and Egypt, the army's LSD experiments with human subjects, and sports. Each report is followed by a discussion in which the teacher elicits evaluative comments from the students. She asks, for instance, "How would you feel about it? Why is it important?" At one point, she makes them aware of how the peace treaty can be related to their earlier study of ancient civilizations. She also asks for more details to clarify issues, and comments on the quality of each presentation and the material presented.

Not Applicable. Feedback possibilities were not inherent in every segment. Segments that basically required children to "take in" or listen to information without the chance for questions or clarification were coded "Not Applicable." The category included most audiovisual segments as well as segments when teachers were giving instructions of a routine nature.

Segment: M063115   Format: Giving Instructions
The teacher announces that story problems will be the focus of the day's work. In one minute she then reviews four steps to be taken leading to the solution. The children are advised to do three of them mentally to set up the problem. The fourth step, the operation, is to be done on paper or on the chalkboard and will lead to the answer. The class quietly listens.

Segment SS211221 in the student behavior section is an example.

Textbook Only. This code assumes the textbook, workbook, or worksheet to be a potential source of feedback. As such it has answers to questions, which is often the case in social studies texts. Math books may provide explicit illustrations of problem solutions on the same page as the student problems or on the previous page. When children work on review sections in mathematics textbooks that indicate where to find more information on how to solve the problem, this code applies, too. The code does not apply when the books do not contain explanations, illustrations, or information to be used in solving problems.

Segment: M061109   Format: Diverse Seatwork
In this segment, students are to complete a math assignment in the textbook and then go on finishing work in English and social studies. The math assignment requires the students to sum two and three fractions, changing the answers to mixed numerals. The example of how to change improper fractions to mixed numerals is given on the opposite page, while three examples of addition appear on the same page in the book. During the seatwork the teacher is sitting at her desk eating lunch. She gets up once and leaves the room for four minutes to reprimand a student. Other than that she does not interact with her students.

Segment: SS061205   Format: Test
This class takes an open book social studies test on the Rocky Mountain States. The teacher disregards any type of questions students pose. Instructions on what to do when finished with the test were given earlier.

EXPECTED STUDENT INTERACTION

These codes for interaction refer to the amount of student interaction expected by the teacher in the instructional activity or the actual level of student interaction. Four levels of interaction are coded for both expected and actual activity. The following code description refers specifically to expected interaction.

None. No interaction between students is expected. They are to work individually.

Segment M041302 in the cognitive level section is an example.

Low. Low levels of interaction are permitted. All interactions are supposed to be work related and nondisruptive. For instance, the students may occasionally whisper to their neighbors to get help on an assignment.

Segment SS211408 in the cognitive level section is an example.

Medium. Interaction is permitted but not necessary. The students are allowed to work together if they wish to do so. They are free to talk to one another. Some students may work by themselves; others will work together and openly communicate.

Segment SS071202 in the cognitive level section is an example.

High. Interaction between students is expected. It is required for the instructional activity. This code is typical for group work.

Segment SS081215 in the cognitive level section is an example.

TASK OPTIONS

Options refer to choices with regard to what to do and with regard to the timing of activity. A teacher may assign a task but tell the children it may be done at any time during the day. A teacher may assign a task and expect it to be done by all children at a given time. A teacher may assign a task which can be done in a variety of ways and allow the child choice regarding the specific way to do it. A teacher may allow a child to select from a variety of tasks and/or to decide on the order in which to pursue them. These various possibilities are covered in the following categories.

Teacher Control—Task and Timing. The teacher assigns a task to be done at a specified time. The assignment may include a small element of choice—for example, which of three explorers to write about.

Teacher Control—Task. The teacher assigns a task, but allows the child to decide the time to do it, within limits.

Student Control—Task and Time. The child selects from a variety available *and* decides when to do it or the order to follow.

Student Control—Task. The child selects a task from a variety available to be done at a teacher-specified time.

Student Control—Materials. The child selects materials for a teacher-assigned task at a specified time. The task may be, for example, free reading or doing research for a social studies report.

Teacher Control—Task, Student Control—Materials, Time. The child selects the materials for a teacher assigned task *and* decides when to do it.

Student Control—Order. The child decides the order in which to do tasks which are teacher assigned in a given time block.

Individualized Programming.   The child moves at his or her own rate through a set of objectives, which are teacher prescribed. The objectives may be reached through a variety of tasks chosen by the child.

OPTIONS WHEN DONE

This code refers to the child's options after completing the assigned tasks.

No.   The child has no options: he or she must wait and do nothing until the teacher starts a new activity or assigns another task.

Yes.   The child can pursue a number of specified tasks. The specified tasks are categorized in the following way:
1. Options are related to the subject taught; for example, an additional math worksheet.
2. Options are unfinished work in any subject matter.
3. Nonacademic games.
4. Reading.
5. Other.

STUDENT LOCATION

Desks.   The students are at their desks or in other designated seating arrangements. This code also applies to situations in which chairs and desks have been moved to facilitate the viewing of films and the like.

Work Tables.   The students are working at work tables.

Floor.   The students are working on the floor.

Rug.   The students are working on the rug.

Office.   The students are working in an office, alcove, laboratory, or other attached yet distinct room.

Hall.   The students are out in the hallway working on some task.

Work Area.   The students are working in classroom areas that are permanently set up as activity centers, such as reading libraries, game centers, living rooms, etc.

Blackboard.   The students in this segment are at the blackboard.

Blackboard/Desks.   One or more students are at the blackboard, while the remainder are at their desks or some other designated work area.

Around Room.   The students may be seen in all or in combinations of the above locations. The code is often applied during instructional situations calling for diverse seatwork or individualized seatwork.

Library.   The students are at the library or media center outside the classroom.

Resource Center.   The students are at the resource or special learning center outside the classroom.

Other Class.   The students are in another classroom.

Other.   The students are at a location not described by any of the above codes.

STUDENT INVOLVEMENT

Off.   Student is daydreaming, wandering around, interacting with one or more peers about non-learning-related matters, or waiting for the teacher to begin or continue the lesson, for teacher feedback, or for the rest of the class to finish. Also code "off" if student is engaged in a learning task that has not been assigned and that you do not think the teacher would permit if he or she were aware of it—e.g., student is doing math during a social studies lecture.

On.   Student is listening attentively, participating in recitations/discussions, working alone on the assigned or permitted task, receiving or giving assistance, or getting ready for the task.

Appendix C
Tables

Table C.1. Number of Instructional Segments, Involvement Segments, Minutes, and Class Periods Observed in Each Class

Teacher[a]	Mathematics Classes				Social Studies Classes			
	Segments	Involvement Segments	Minutes	Periods	Segments	Involvement Segments	Minutes	Periods
A	37	21	456	9	16	16	138	3
	24	24	386	9	16	16	357	9
	26	26	377	9	15	15	349	8
B	33	32	446	9	21	21	319	8
C	23	23	431	9	22	22	305	8
D	27	25	373	9	19	18	378	7
E	39	35	529	10	57	49	680	10
F	26	21	462	10	34	29	434	9
G	27	24	442	10	23	22	379	8
H	21	19	272	9	14	12	310	8
I	34	33	422	10	14	14	251	9
	38	36	528	10	24	24	286	8
	19	15	246	7	36	27	394	9
J	13	11	299	7	37	37	182	6
K	21	21	290	8	21	21	216	7
	23	21	332	8				
L	10	9	271	7	67	61	418	8
M	19	17	287	7	37	31	367	8
N	26	25	376	9	33	31	370	9
O	51	44	450	10	34	22	381	11

[a]Teachers A–O taught classes in both subjects shown on a given row. Other teachers' letters omitted.

Table C.2. Mean Durations of Segments
by Segment Features

Segment Feature[a]	Mathematics		Social Studies	
	$\bar{X}$ Duration	S.D.	$\bar{X}$ Duration	S.D.
Format:				
Uniform Seatwork	21.7	12.0	20.2	11.7
Individualized Seatwork	34.8	10.3	—	—
Diverse Seatwork	30.4	13.7	26.1	11.7
Recitation	16.6	9.4	17.1	11.8
Group Work	39.0	—	23.1	11.6
Contest, Game	21.0	11.4	13.7	7.4
Checking Work	9.8	5.7	11.0	5.5
Giving Instructions	3.8	2.0	5.8	3.2
Task Preparation	4.5	2.2	8.1	2.9
Student Reports	—	—	20.5	12.1
Discussion	15.0	7.1	9.7	7.4
Test	21.1	10.2	24.5	17.6
Lecture	10.1	7.2	12.0	10.8
Demonstration	7.3	1.2	19.6	12.4
Film/Audiovisual	—	—	16.5	10.3
Tutorial	21.5	9.1	—	—
Stocks	—	—	5.0	2.0
Pacing:				
Teacher	13.4	9.1	12.9	10.3
Child	25.1	12.7	22.3	12.7
Cooperative	26.4	12.5	22.9	11.7
Mechanical	—	—	16.5	10.6
Expected student interaction:				
None	18.0	11.7	15.7	12.0
Low	22.1	14.1	15.4	11.1
Medium	28.9	14.3	22.0	11.4
High	25.0	13.3	24.2	11.4
Task options:				
Teacher–Task and Time	16.7	10.9	16.6	12.0
Teacher–Task; Student– Time	23.2	9.0	9.0	—
Student–Task and Time	39.9	8.2	35.2	14.4
Student–Task; Teacher– Time	25.0	6.2	24.5	7.2

(*continued*)

Table C.2.   (*Continued*)

Segment Feature[a]	Mathematics		Social Studies	
	$\overline{X}$ Duration	S.D.	$\overline{X}$ Duration	S.D.
Task options, *cont.*				
Teacher–Task and Time;				
Student–Materials	41.5	17.7	23.9	8.6
Teacher–Task and Time;				
Student–Order	26.8	11.4	16.8	2.6
Individualized Program	34.8	10.3	—	—
Student location:				
Desks	17.5	12.0	16.6	11.8
Blackboard/Desks	17.2	9.4	—	—
Office	32.5	11.0	—	—
Work Area	30.7	10.6	30.4	11.5
Work Tables	—	—	25.0	7.7
Rug	—	—	18.6	9.8
Established Area[b]	—	—	11.5	10.2
Library	—	—	27.1	12.2
Resource Center	38.8	13.0	—	—
Other (<1%)	19.0	12.3	20.7	10.9
Feedback:				
Teacher–Low	16.3	10.9	17.4	11.2
Teacher–High	18.3	10.3	15.3	14.1
None	14.0	10.9	13.3	11.8
Student Feedback	24.7	11.3	25.3	13.2
Textbook Only	23.0	10.9	17.5	12.8
Not Applicable	3.9	2.1	10.5	9.4
Additional materials:				
Manipulatives	28.6	10.2	17.0	14.0
Books	29.0	—	24.6	10.6
Self-Check	29.3	17.6	17.0	9.5
Teacher–Low and				
Textbook	23.2	12.2	20.5	12.2
Teacher–Low and Addi-				
tional materials	25.2	12.7	17.5	8.5
Teacher–High and Addi-				
tional materials	23.4	14.5	26.5	18.0

(*continued*)

Table C.2. (*Continued*)

| Segment Feature[a] | Mathematics | | Social Studies | |
	$\overline{X}$ Duration	S.D.	$\overline{X}$ Duration	S.D.
Cognitive level:				
Not Cognitive	—	—	28.9	9.6
Receive/Recall Facts	9.4	8.6	12.6	10.2
Concepts and Skills	21.6	12.3	21.1	11.9
Research Skills A:				
Locate Information	—	—	26.4	10.5
Research Skills B:				
Symbolic/Graphic	—	—	19.1	15.2
Application	18.8	9.9	18.2	8.9
Other Higher Mental				
Processes	12.0	—	18.6	13.6
Teacher role:				
Watcher/Helper–Intermittent	25.2	11.6	23.1	11.4
Watcher/Helper–Continuous	30.9	11.4	23.4	12.3
Recitation Leader	15.7	9.1	15.2	11.4
Not in Segment	26.0	14.3	16.3	11.6
Action Director	8.4	6.3	12.8	10.7
Instructor	6.7	5.9	9.5	7.8
Reader	9.7	7.3	8.1	5.4
Tester	18.9	8.3	29.3	16.3

[a]Features are defined in appendix B.
[b]Students are working in an area set up specifically for the activity in which they are engaged.

Notes

CHAPTER 1

1. Ozcelik (1973), in one of the few studies using both overt and covert measures of student involvement, found a positive association between the two measures, but also considerable independence in teacher-led settings. See Wittrock (1986) for a review of research on students' thought processes during instruction.

2. The same properties are associated with more attention in infants (Kagan 1971).

CHAPTER 2

1. As explained in the preface, J. Alan Thomas and I obtained funds to collect data jointly. Consequently, criteria for sample selection were established collaboratively in order to meet the research goals of both of us.

To select the sample, all districts in the Chicago area were stratified by school expenditure levels and community socioeconomic status. Districts in the upper third or lower third of expenditures per pupil in the state of Illinois were studied. District expenditure levels were determined from information reported by the Illinois Office of Education for the 1976–77 school year. Districts were tentatively placed into low-, middle- or high-SES categories based on 1970 census data on median family income in the district. Six possible cells from which to select school districts were created by combining the two categories of expenditure level and the three categories of socioeconomic status. However, only five combinations described actual schools: there were no low expenditure, high-SES schools.

Districts were randomly sampled from the five cells. If a district refused to participate, a substitute district with similar characteristics was identified. In all but two cases, the substitute districts were selected randomly.

Sampling information was checked for accuracy in the schools and classrooms included in the study. The socioeconomic characteristics of several classrooms differed from the 1970 census information. More accurate information was obtained from lists of the occupations of the heads of households in the classes we studied. Prestige rankings of occupations were used to place schools and districts in their proper sample position.

2. Random selection was used in sampling districts and in selecting students for study. Nevertheless, some volunteer bias is present in our sample since districts, teachers, parents, and students had to agree to participate once selected. Willingness to participate probably resulted in schools and classes that were somewhat more excellent (as judged by each school's standards) or more interested in educational research than a completely random sample.

3. The parent interview was used by Thomas and his colleagues.

4. A complete description of the other information we collected is provided in Thomas and Kemmerer (1983) and Stodolsky (1983).

5. The teacher interviews were developed and conducted by Plihal (1982).

6. Two half-day narrative records were collected during the first week to provide background on the experience of the classroom group in all subjects. The records also contained descriptions of classroom activities and procedures useful for understanding our observations in math and social studies.

7. Every record was segmented by one of us and checked by the other. Initial agreement was achieved on about 90 percent of the records. Difficult cases occurred primarily in classes with many simultaneous activities and when teachers themselves were unclear in setting boundaries of activities. The two coders discussed these cases and together determined final segment designations.

8. To assess coding reliability, two analysts independently coded twenty randomly selected segments from each subject area. On thirty-one variables coded (fifteen activity structure variables and the materials codes), 92.4 percent agreement was reached (social studies = 91.3, math = 93.4). No variable produced less than 70 percent agreement.

9. A full discussion of sources of interdependence in the study data is provided in Stodolsky (1983).

CHAPTER 3

1. Summary descriptions of each class can be found in appendix C of Stodolsky (1983).

2. The format used to study stock market activity did not fit easily into the general format categories. The teacher read stock values in response to student requests, students charted values and made price comparisons, and the group periodically discussed economic trends and market conditions. Sometimes the activity resembled a dictation, but that characterization does not capture all its aspects. Placement of the segments in social studies was

somewhat arbitrary given the integrated content, but this was the only unambiguous case of subject matter integration we noted.

3. Others (e.g., Barr and Dreeben 1983) use *pacing* to refer to the amount of content covered in relation to instructional time.

4. Of the child-paced math segments, 80 percent had no social interaction, 12.9 percent had low interaction, and 7.1 percent had high interaction levels. Of the child-paced social studies segments, 69.8 percent had no social interaction, 20.7 percent had low interaction levels, 4.7 percent had medium levels, and 4.7 percent had high levels of interaction. Of teacher-paced math segments, 94.3 percent had no social interaction, 4.5 percent had low levels, 0.8 percent medium levels, and 0.4 percent high levels. Of teacher-paced social studies segments, 86.7 percent had no social interaction, 11.5 percent had low interaction levels, and 1.8 percent had medium levels of interaction.

5. The adequacy of textbooks in providing feedback will be discussed later.

6. A complete list of all segment patterns is available from the author.

7. The term *traditional* is used to capture a common instructional pattern that has been used over many decades in American elementary schools. The main ingredients, as described in the text, are the extensive use of whole-class recitation and seatwork, teacher direction of lessons or teacher specification of the tasks children pursue, and uniform expectations for pupils. The math and social studies classes grouped as traditional look rather similar, especially in instructional format, but there are important subject matter differences in many other segment features. Classes in each subject that are not traditional also follow distinct instructional programs (i.e., individualized math classes and group-work social studies classes).

In general, the term *traditional* and others such as *progressive* or *modern* are meant to convey information about practice or ideology, not to indicate a value judgment. When I want to communicate a value statement, it will be clearly indicated.

CHAPTER 4

1. Factors besides setting properties also affect involvement. In individual students, these include learning histories, various abilities and interests, and such transient conditions as the student's state of physical comfort and health. In our sample, average involvement in math classes is significantly correlated with math test averages ($r = .62$, $p < .01$), but in social studies classes there is no correlation between reading test performance and average involvement. Classroom SES does not correlate with average classroom involvement levels in either subject.

Berliner (1983) has suggested a research program to investigate how student aptitudes and activity structures interact. However, in our research the average response of groups of students to multiple instances of settings with a given property is assumed to reflect a typical response to the setting property, with individual factors largely canceling one another out.

2. See the section in chapter 5 on the existential fallacy in educational research for my views on this issue.

3. For this analysis, mechanical pacing has been eliminated because we had so few segments in our sample.

4. Average involvement in the sample classes did vary substantially. Class means ranged from .53 to .93 in social studies, from .62 to .88 in math. A one-way analysis of variance on average involvement level in math classes and social studies classes separately showed that classes differ significantly in involvement in both subjects ($F = 5.71$, $p < .001$ for math; $F = 6.88$, $p < .001$ for social studies). Differences among classes do not relate to the sampling variables of SES or expenditure levels.

5. If tasks are much too difficult for children, their ability to be involved will be impaired by anxiety, confusion, or despair.

6. A Duncan's multiple-range test indicates that the teacher-paced segments have a significantly lower average involvement than the cooperative and child-paced segments.

7. A possible methodological explanation for this finding merits discussion. The expected work patterns under different pacing conditions vary, and some problems in observer accuracy may arise.

In a small-group setting, interactions between children are an expected part of the work pattern, whereas in most child- and teacher-paced segments, interactions between children are not sanctioned. An observer noting an interaction between children under child pacing or teacher pacing is likely to assume the interaction is off-task, unless evidence to the contrary presents itself. Similarly, in the small-group setting, an observer would be likely to assume that interaction was work-related unless confronted with evidence that it was socializing or off-task. Giving children the "benefit of the doubt" in the small-group setting might account for the somewhat higher on-task rates in these segments.

Can this possible source of bias in our data be eliminated? A number of points suggest that it is not a major bias, but it is not possible to totally rule it out. First, acceptable levels of reliability were achieved among observers. In many cases, but not all, the observer was able actually to hear the contents of the interactions, and these are recorded on the time sampling sheets. Inferences when the observer could not hear accurately—the only source of potential problems—form a relatively small subset of all observations. In other pacing conditions, observer locations were sometimes not ideal, and best guesses were made from general nonverbal and bodily cues. Similar inferences were made recording interactions in small groups.

The strongest argument against methodological bias seems to be the fact that systematic trends within group-work segments can be detected. In particular, as we will see in the succeeding section, cognitive-level differences in group-work tasks are associated with more or less student involvement. The emergence of these differences supports the idea that in most cases observers were in fact able to distinguish work-related from socializing episodes in the groups.

8. A detailed analysis of the cooperative segments is available in Graybeal and Stodolsky (1985).

9. A one-way ANOVA on the four pacing conditions in social studies shows a significant effect ($F = 5.48, p < .001$). A Duncan's multiple-range test shows that the cooperative segments have a significantly higher average involvement than the other three pacing conditions, which are not statistically different from one another.

10. The rather large standard deviations associated with the average involvement estimates, particularly for the math preparatory segments, should be noted here. The variation is likely to be a function of some methodological features as well as real disparities in student response to preparatory segments. In particular, the segments are very short, and since the involvement estimates are based on relatively few observation occasions, they are likely to be unstable. In addition, a number of the averages in table 4.4 are based on a small number of segments—another feature that would contribute to instability and inaccuracy in estimating population variation with the sample standard deviations.

11. In the schools studied here, there is no relationship between SES of district and curricular program in either subject. There seems to be some tendency for individualized math and group work to occur more often in both the highest and lowest SES districts and least often in the districts with lower-middle SES. Thomas and Kemmerer (1983), however, did find that individualized math programs were more likely to be used in high SES districts than low SES districts. Their sample included our schools as well as others.

12. Increments in on-task behavior at any point on the scale are not of equal value for learning. A class in which students are engaged in activity around 60 percent of the time is very different from one in which children are involved 80 percent of the time. A 10 percentage point increase in student attention in both settings will not have similar consequences for student learning or for the tone of the educational environment.

13. The primary reasons for this conclusion will be noted here. (See Perrone [1975] for other cogent objections.) Standardized achievement tests are constructed to sample objectives from a variety of curricular approaches. Since the tests are constructed to appeal to a national market, items are developed to coordinate with a variety of topics, only some of which are included in any particular textbook or class program. In a recent study, researchers at Michigan State analyzed fourth-grade mathematics

tests and widely used textbooks. They found a maximum of 50 percent overlap between the test item content and what was taught in a given textbook (Freeman et al. 1980). Elementary school math is much more uniform in its content and objectives than other subjects. Nevertheless, available tests would be a poor match to any given instructional program organized around a textbook. As our research confirms, social studies subject matter is much more diverse, and little concordance between curriculum content and any general test could be expected.

CHAPTER 5

1. It is easy to overstate the ease and success with which students can derive information from elementary social studies and science texts. Mosenthal (1983) has found that while the information to answer questions posed in the textbooks is usually provided, the information may not be adequately structured for students by the books or by their teachers. Both Mosenthal (1983) and Armbruster (1984) find that some textbooks do not adequately prepare students to comprehend main ideas and answer questions beyond the factual level. Other textbooks seem very adequate for student learning and comprehension.

2. Glaessner and I are analyzing interviews with other fifth graders about learning math and social studies with support from the Benton Center for Curriculum and Instruction, University of Chicago.

3. The effect that the setting has on both teachers and students is a topic worthy of further study. Within that area, one might ask whether the teachers who create the environments are aware of the ways in which they both limit and extend opportunities for learning. For example, a particular type of activity structure directs attention to certain features of children's learning and behavior and sets particular standards of acceptable behavior. Strengths and weaknesses in students are perceived in terms of the particular program used. Similarly, teachers' skills and abilities are used to different degrees depending on the instructional program. Do teachers see themselves and students as fairly consistent across learning environments, or do they recognize that classrooms shape and select certain behaviors?

4. The existential fallacy is similar to the naturalistic fallacy and is usually attributed to Hume, who discussed it in his *Treatise,* although it was given its name by G. E. Moore in 1903. Not everyone concedes that it is in fact a fallacy to take what is ordinarily the case and consider it obligatory (Runes 1942).

References

Adams, R. S., and B. J. Biddle. 1970. *Realities of teaching: Exploration with videotape.* New York: Holt, Rinehart and Winston.

Anderson, L. M., N. L. Brubaker, J. Alleman-Brooks, and G. G. Duffy. 1985. A qualitative study of seatwork in first-grade classrooms. *Elementary School Journal* 86:123–40.

Anderson, L. W. 1984. Attention, tasks and time. In *Time and school learning,* ed. L. W. Anderson. London: Croom Helm.

Arlin, M. 1979. Teacher transitions can disrupt time flow in classrooms. *American Educational Research Journal* 16:42–56.

Armbruster, B. B. 1984. The problem of "inconsiderate text." In *Comprehension instruction: Perspectives and suggestions,* ed. G. G. Duffy, L. R. Roehler, and J. Mason. New York: Longman.

Barker, R. G. 1968. *Ecological psychology: Concepts and methods for studying the environment of human behavior.* Stanford, Calif.: Stanford University Press.

Barr, R., and R. Dreeben, with N. Wiratchai. 1983. *How schools work.* Chicago: University of Chicago Press.

Bell, M., and J. Bell. 1983. *Counting, numeration, and operation capabilities of a group of suburban primary school children: A descriptive report.* Report no. G-80-0099. Washington, D.C.: National Institute for Education.

Berger, P. L., and T. Luckmann. 1966. *The social construction of reality: A treatise in the sociology of knowledge.* Garden City, N.Y.: Doubleday.

Berliner, D. C. 1979. Tempus Educare. In *Research on teaching: Concepts, findings and implications,* ed. P. L. Peterson and H. J. Walberg. Berkeley, Calif.: McCutchan.

Berliner, D. C. 1983. Developing conceptions of classroom environments: Some light on the T in classroom studies of ATI. *Educational Psychologist* 18, no. 1:1–13.

Bloom, B. S., M. D. Engelhart, E. J. Furst, W. H. Hill, and D. R. Krathwohl. 1956. *Taxonomy of educational objectives: The classification of educational goals.* Handbook 1, *Cognitive domain.* New York: Longmans Green.

181

Bloom, S. 1976. *Peer and cross-age tutoring in the schools*. Washington, D.C.: National Institute of Education.

Blumenfeld, P. C., J. Mergendoller, and D. Swarthout. 1987. Tasks as heuristics for understanding: Student learning and motivation. *Journal of Curriculum Studies* 19:134–47.

Blumenfeld, P. C., P. R. Pintrich, J. Meece, and K. Wessels. 1982. The formation and role of self perceptions of ability in elementary classrooms. *Elementary School Journal* 82:401–20.

Bossert, S. T. 1979. *Tasks and social relationships in classrooms*. New York: Cambridge University Press.

Breer, P. E., and E. A. Locke. 1965. *Task experience as a source of attitudes*. Homewood, Ill.: Dorsey Press.

Brophy, J. E., and T. L. Good. 1974. *Teacher-student relationships: Causes and consequences*. New York: Holt, Rinehart and Winston.

Brophy, J. E., and T. L. Good. 1986. Teacher behavior and student achievement. In *Handbook of research on teaching*, 3d ed., ed. M. C. Wittrock. New York: Macmillan.

Brush, L. R. 1980. *Encouraging girls in mathematics: The problem and solution*. Cambridge, Mass.: Abt Books.

Burns, R. B. 1984. How time is used in elementary schools: The activity structure of classrooms. In *Time and school learning*, ed. L. W. Anderson. London: Croom Helm.

Buros, O. K. 1977. Fifty years in testing: Some reminiscences, criticisms and suggestions. *Educational Researcher*, July, 9–15.

Bussis, A. M., E. A. Chittenden, and M. Amarel. 1976. *Beyond surface curriculum*. Boulder, Colo.: Westview Press.

Carey, S. 1985. *Conceptual change in childhood*. Cambridge: MIT Press.

Carpenter, T. P., M. K. Corbitt, H. S. Kepner, M. M. Lindquist, and R. E. Reys. 1981. *Results from the second mathematics assessment of the National Assessment of Educational Progress*. Reston, Va.: National Council of Teachers of Mathematics.

Chall, J. 1967. *Learning to read: The great debate*. New York: McGraw-Hill.

Chall, J. 1977. *Reading 1967–1977: A decade of change and promise*. Bloomington, Ind.: Phi Delta Kappa.

Church, R. L., and M. W. Sedlak. 1976. *Education in the United States. An interpretive history*. New York: Free Press.

Clark, C. M., and P. L. Peterson. 1984. *Teachers' thought processes*. Occasional paper no. 72. East Lansing, Mich.: Michigan State University, Institute for Research on Teaching.

Clark, C. M., and P. L. Peterson. 1986. Teachers' thought processes. In *Handbook of research on teaching*, 3d ed., ed. M. C. Wittrock. New York: Macmillan.

Clark, C. M., and R. J. Yinger. 1979. Teachers' thinking. In *Research on teaching: Concepts, findings and implications,* ed. P. L. Peterson and H. J. Walberg. Berkeley, Calif.: McCutchan.

Cohen, E. G. 1984. Talking and working together: Status, interaction and learning. In *The social context of instruction: Group organization and group processes,* ed. P. L. Peterson, L. C. Wilkinson, and M. T. Hallinan. New York: Academic Press.

Cuban, L. 1984. *How teachers taught: Constancy and change in American classrooms 1890–1980.* New York: Longman.

Davidson, N. 1980. The small group discovery method: 1967–1977. In *Problem solving studies in mathematics,* ed. J. G. Harvey and T. A. Romberg. Madison: Wisconsin Research and Development Center for Individualized Schooling.

Dewey, J. 1899. *The school and society.* Chicago: University of Chicago Press.

Doyle, W. 1977. Paradigms for research on teacher effectiveness. In *Review of Research in Education,* vol. 5, ed. L. S. Shulman. Itasca, Ill.: Peacock Publishers.

Doyle, W. 1983. Academic work. *Review of Educational Research* 53:159–99.

Dreeben, R. 1968. *On what is learned in school.* Reading, Mass.: Addison-Wesley.

Dunkin, M., and B. Biddle. 1974. *The study of teaching.* New York: Holt, Rinehart and Winston.

Durkin, D. 1984. Is there a match between what elementary teachers do and what basal reader manuals recommend? *The Reading Teacher* 37:734–44.

Elbaz, F. 1983. *Teacher thinking: A study of practical knowledge.* New York: Nichols.

Ellis, A. K. 1981. *Teaching and learning elementary social studies.* Boston: Allyn and Bacon.

Erickson, F. 1986. Qualitative methods in research on teaching. *Handbook of research on teaching,* 3d ed., ed. M. C. Wittrock. New York: Macmillan.

Evertson, C. M., and J. L. Green. 1986. Observation as inquiry and method. In *Handbook of research on teaching,* 3d ed., ed. M. C. Wittrock. New York: Macmillan.

Feiman-Nemser, S. 1983. Learning to teach. In *Handbook of teaching and policy,* ed. L. S. Shulman and G. Sykes. New York: Longman.

Ferguson, T. L. 1984. *School level resource allocation decisions.* Ph.D. diss., University of Chicago.

Fey, J. T. 1979. Mathematics teaching today: Perspectives from three national surveys. *Arithmetic Teacher* 27, no. 2: 10–14.

Fisher, L. W., N. N. Filby, R. S. Marliave, L. S. Cahen, M. M. Dishaw,

J. E. Moore, and D. C. Berliner. 1978. *Teaching behaviors, academic learning time and student achievement: Final report of phase III-B, beginning teacher evaluation study.* San Francisco: Far West Laboratory for Education Research and Development.

Flanders, J. 1987. How much of the content of mathematics textbooks is new? *Arithmetic Teacher* 35, no. 1: 18–23.

Flanders, N. A. Teacher influence in the classroom. 1967. In *Interaction analysis: Theory, research and application,* ed. E. J. Amidon and J. B. Hough. Reading, Mass.: Addison-Wesley.

Floden, R., A. C. Porter, W. H. Schmidt, D. J. Freeman, and J. R. Schwille. 1981. Responses to curriculum pressures: A policy-capturing study of teacher decisions about content. *Journal of Educational Psychology* 73:129–41.

Freeman, D. J., T. M. Kuhs, A. C. Porter, L. B. Knappen, R. E. Floden, W. H. Schmidt, and J. R. Schwille. 1980. *The fourth-grade mathematics curriculum as inferred from textbooks and tests.* Research series no. 82. East Lansing, Mich.: Michigan State University, Institute for Research on Teaching. ERIC Document Reproduction Service no. ED 199-047.

Freeman, F. N. 1916. *The psychology of the common branches.* New York: Houghton Mifflin.

Fullan, M., and A. Pomfret. 1977. Research on curriculum and instruction implementation. *Review of Educational Research* 47:335–97.

Gage, N. L. 1978. *The scientific basis of the art of teaching.* New York: Teachers College Press.

Gall, M. D. 1970. The use of questions in teaching. *Review of Educational Research* 40:707–20.

Giaconia, R. M., and L. V. Hedges. 1982. Identifying features of effective open education. *Review of Educational Research* 52, no. 4:579–602.

Glaessner, B. E. 1986. Math and social studies: What do fourth and fifth graders think they are and how do they feel about them? Unpublished trial research paper, University of Chicago.

Goffman, E. 1959. *The presentation of self in everyday life.* Garden City, N.Y.: Doubleday, Anchor.

Good, T. L., D. A. Grouws, and H. Ebmeier. 1983. *Active mathematics teaching.* New York: Longman.

Goodlad, J. I. 1984. *A place called school.* New York: McGraw-Hill.

Grannis, J. C. 1975. Community, competence, and individuation: The effects of different controls in educational environments. *IRCD Bulletin* 10, no. 2: 1–18.

Grannis, J. C. 1978. Task engagement and the consistency of pedagogical controls: An ecological study of differently structured classroom settings. *Curriculum Inquiry* 8:3–37.

Grannis, J. C., and E. Jackson. 1973. *Columbia classroom environments.* Project final report, contract no. OEC-O-71-0593. New York: Institute for Pedagogical Studies, Teachers College, Columbia University. Mimeo.

Graybeal, S. S. In preparation. *Assumptions about instructional practice in fifth-grade math and social studies textbooks and teacher's guides.* Ph.D. diss., University of Chicago.

Graybeal, S. S., and S. S. Stodolsky. 1985. Peer work groups in elementary schools. *American Journal of Education* 93:409–28.

Graybeal, S. S., and S. S. Stodolsky. 1986. Instructional practice in fifth-grade math and social studies: An analysis of teacher's guides. Paper presented at annual meeting of American Educational Research Association.

Graybeal, S. S., and S. S. Stodolsky. 1987. Where's all the "good stuff"? An analysis of fifth-grade math and social studies teacher's guides. Paper presented at annual meeting of American Educational Research Association.

Greeno, J. G. 1978. Understanding and procedural knowledge in mathematics instruction. *Educational Psychologist* 12:262–83.

Gump, P. V. 1967. *The classroom behavior setting: Its nature and relation to student behavior.* Final report, U.S. Office of Education project no. 2453. Lawrence: University of Kansas Press.

Gump, P. V. 1982. School settings and their keeping. In *Helping teachers manage classrooms,* ed. D. L. Duke. Alexandria, Va.: Association for Supervision and Curriculum Development.

Haney, W. 1984. Testing reasoning and reasoning about testing. *Review of Educational Research* 54:597–654.

Hawkins, D. 1974. *The informed vision: Essays on learning and human nature.* New York: Schocken.

Hoetker, A. J., and W. P. Ahlbrand. 1969. The persistence of the recitation. *American Educational Research Journal* 6:145–67.

Horwitz, R. A. 1979. Psychological effects of the "open classroom." *Review of Educational Research* 49:71–86.

Hoyles, C. 1982. The pupil's view of mathematics learning. *Educational Studies in Mathematics* 13:349–72.

Husen, T. 1967. *International study of achievement in mathematics: A comparison of twelve countries.* New York: Wiley.

Jackson, P. W. 1968. *Life in classrooms.* New York: Holt, Rinehart and Winston.

Jackson, P. W. 1986. *The practice of teaching.* New York: Teachers College Press.

Jarolimek, J. 1977. *Social studies in elementary education.* 5th ed. New York: Macmillan.

Jarolimek, J. 1981. The social studies: An overview. In *The social studies.* Part 2 of Eightieth yearbook of the National Society for the Study of Education. Chicago: University of Chicago Press.

Kagan, J. 1971. *Change and continuity in infancy.* New York: Wiley.

Kluckhohn, C. 1961. Universal categories of culture. In *Readings in cross-cultural methodology,* ed. F. Moore. New Haven: HRAF Press.

Kounin, J. S. 1970. *Discipline and group management in classrooms.* New York: Holt, Rinehart and Winston.

Kounin, J. S., and P. V. Gump. 1974. Signal systems of lesson settings and the task-related behavior of preschool children. *Journal of Educational Psychology* 66:554–62.

Krammer, H. P. 1985. The textbook as classroom context variable. *Teaching and Teacher Education* 1, no. 4:273–78.

Leinhardt, G. 1983. Novice and expert knowledge of individual students' achievement. *Educational Psychologist* 18:165–79.

Luchins, A. S. 1942. Mechanization in problem solving: The effect of Einstellung. *Psychological Monographs* 54, no. 6:whole no. 428.

Madaus, G. F., P. W. Airasian, and T. Kellaghan. 1980. *School effectiveness: A reassessment of the evidence.* New York: McGraw-Hill.

Man: A course of study. 1968. Cambridge, Mass.: Education Development Center, Inc.

Man and his world: Many Americans—one nation, teacher's ed. 1974. New York: Noble and Noble.

Marshall, H., and R. Weinstein. 1984. Classroom factors affecting students' self-evaluations: An interactional model. *Review of Educational Research* 54:301–25.

Marton, F., and R. Saljo. 1976. On qualitative differences in learning. Part 2, Outcomes as a function of the learner's conception of the task. *British Journal of Educational Psychology* 46:115–27.

Mead, G. H. 1934. *Mind, self, and society.* Chicago: University of Chicago Press.

Medley, D. M., and H. E. Mitzel. 1963. Measuring classroom behavior by systematic observation. In *Handbook of research on teaching,* ed. N. L. Gage. Chicago: Rand McNally.

Minuchin, P., B. Biber, E. Shapiro, and H. Zimiles. 1969. *The psychological impact of school experience: A comparative study of nine-year-old children in contrasting schools.* New York: Basic Books.

Morrissett, I., ed. 1982. *Social studies in the 1980's: A report of project SPAN.* Alexandria, Va.: Association for Supervision and Curriculum Development.

Mosenthal, J. 1983. *Instruction in the interpretation of a writer's argument.* Ph.D. diss., University of Illinois, Urbana.

National Advisory Committee on Mathematical Education (NACOME). 1975. *Overview and analysis of school mathematics: K–12.* Washington, D.C.: Conference Board of the Mathematical Sciences.

Nicely, R. F., Jr. 1985. Higher-order thinking skills in mathematics textbooks. *Educational Leadership,* Apr., 26–30.

Orlandi, L. R. 1971. Evaluation of learning in secondary school social studies. In *Handbook on formative and summative evaluation of student learning*, ed. B. S. Bloom, J. T. Hastings, and G. Madaus. New York: McGraw-Hill.

Ozcelik, D. A. 1973. *Student involvement in the learning process*. Ph.D. diss., University of Chicago.

Perrone, V. 1975. *Testing and evaluation: New views*. Washington, D.C.: Association for Childhood Education International.

Pipho, C. 1977. Minimal competency testing: A look at state standards. *Educational Leadership* 34:516–20.

Plihal, J. E. 1982. *Intrinsic rewards of teaching*. Ph.D. diss., University of Chicago.

Posner, G. 1982. A cognitive science conception of curriculum and instruction. *Journal of Curriculum Studies* 14:343–51.

Raizen, S. A., and L. V. Jones, eds. 1985. *Indicators of precollege education in science and mathematics: A preliminary review*. Washington, D.C.: National Academy Press.

Romberg, T. A., and T. P. Carpenter. 1986. Research on teaching and learning mathematics: Two disciplines of scientific inquiry. In *Handbook of research on teaching*, 3d ed., ed. M. C. Wittrock. New York: Macmillan.

Rosenholtz, S. J., and B. Wilson. 1980. The effect of classroom structure on shared perceptions of ability. *American Educational Research Journal* 17:75–82.

Rosenshine, B. V. 1976. Classroom instruction. In *The psychology of teaching methods*. Part 1 of Seventy-fifth yearbook of the National Society for the Study of Education. Chicago: University of Chicago Press.

Rosenshine, B. V. 1979. Content, time, and direct instruction. In *Research on teaching: Concepts, findings and implications*, ed. P. L. Peterson and H. J. Walberg. Berkeley, Calif.: McCutchan.

Rosenshine, B. V. 1980. How time is spent in elementary classrooms. In *Time to Learn*, ed. C. Denham and A. Lieberman. Washington, D.C.: National Institute of Education.

Ross, R. P. 1984. Classroom segments: The structuring of school time. In *Time and school learning*, ed. L. W. Anderson. London: Croom Helm.

Runes, D. D., ed. 1942. *The dictionary of philosophy*. New York: Philosophical Library.

Salomon, G. 1983. The differential investment of mental effort in learning from different sources. *Educational Psychologist* 18:42–50.

Schoenfeld, A. H. 1983. Beyond the purely cognitive: Belief systems, social cognitions, and metacognitions as driving forces in intellectual performance. *Cognitive Science* 7:329–63.

Schwille, J., A. Porter, G. Belli, R. Floden, D. Freeman, L. Knappen, T.

Kuhs, and W. Schmidt. 1983. Teachers as policy brokers in the content of elementary school mathematics. In *Handbook of teaching and policy*, ed. L. S. Shulman and G. Sykes. New York: Longman.

Shapiro, E. 1973. Educational evaluation: Rethinking the criteria of competence. *School Review* 81, no. 4:523–50.

Sharan, S., P. Hare, C. D. Webb, and R. Hertz-Lazarowitz, eds. 1980. *Cooperation in education*. Provo, Utah: Brigham Young Press.

Shavelson, R. J., and P. Stern. 1981. Research on teachers' pedagogical thoughts, judgments, decisions, and behavior. *Review of Educational Research* 51:455–98.

Shulman, L. S. 1974. The psychology of school subjects: A premature obituary? *Journal of Research in Science Teaching* 11:319–39.

Shulman, L. S. 1986. Paradigms and research programs in the study of teaching: A contemporary perspective. In *Handbook of research on teaching*, 3d ed., ed. M. C. Wittrock. New York: Macmillan.

Silver, E. A., ed. 1985. *Teaching and learning mathematical problem solving: Multiple research perspectives*. Hillsdale, N.J.: Lawrence Erlbaum Associates.

Sirotnik, K. A. 1983. What you see is what you get: Consistency, persistency, and mediocrity in classrooms. *Harvard Educational Review* 53, no. 1:16–31.

Slavin, R. E. 1980. Cooperative learning. *Review of Educational Research* 50:315–42.

Slavin, R. E. 1983. *Cooperative learning*. New York: Longman.

Slavin, R. E., M. Leavey, and N. A. Madden. 1984. Combining cooperative learning and individualized instruction: Effects on student mathematics achievement, attitudes and behaviors. *Elementary School Journal* 84:409–22.

Soar, R. S., and R. M. Soar. 1976. An attempt to identify measures of teacher effectiveness from four studies. *Journal of Teacher Education* 27:261–67.

Squire, J. R. 1987. Studies of textbooks: Are we asking the right questions? Paper presented at Inaugural Conference of the Benton Center for Curriculum and Instruction, University of Chicago.

Stake, R. E., and J. Easley, eds. 1978. *Case studies in science education*. Vol. 2, *Design, overview and general findings*. SE 78-74 vol. 2, National Science Foundation contract no. C 7621134. Washington, D.C.: U.S. Government Printing Office.

Stallings, J. 1975. Implementation and child effects of teaching practices in Follow Through classrooms. *Society for Research in Child Development Monograph* 40, nos. 7–8, Serial No. 163.

Stallings, J., and D. Kaskowitz. 1974. *Follow Through classroom observation evaluation 1972–1973*. Stanford Research Institute project URU-7370. Menlo Park, Calif.: Stanford Research Institute.

Stano, S. A. 1981. *A study of the relationship between teaching techniques and student achievement on higher cognitive level question asking skills.* Ph.D. diss., University of Chicago.

Stigler, J. W., K. C. Fuson, M. Ham, and M. S. Kim. 1986. An analysis of addition and subtraction word problems in American and Soviet elementary mathematics textbooks. *Cognition and Instruction* 3, no. 3: 153–71.

Stigler, J. W., S. Lee, G. W. Lucker, and H. Stevenson. 1982. Curriculum and achievement in mathematics: A study of elementary school children in Japan, Taiwan, and the United States. *Journal of Educational Psychology* 74:315–22.

Stodolsky, S. S. 1972. Defining treatment and outcome in early childhood education. In *Rethinking urban education*, ed. H. Walberg and A. Kopan. San Francisco: Jossey-Bass.

Stodolsky, S. S. 1983. *Classroom activity structures in the fifth grade.* Final report, National Institute of Education contract no. 400-77-0094. Chicago: University of Chicago. ERIC no. ED242 412.

Stodolsky, S. S. 1984a. Frameworks for studying instructional processes in peer work groups. In *The social context of instruction: Group organization and group processes*, ed. P. L. Peterson, L. C. Wilkinson, and M. T. Hallinan. New York: Academic Press.

Stodolsky, S. S. 1984b. Teacher evaluation: The limits of looking. *Educational Researcher* 13, no. 9:11–18.

Stodolsky, S. S. 1985. Telling math: Origins of math aversion and anxiety. *Educational Psychologist* 20, no. 3:125–33.

Stodolsky, S. S. 1986. *Origins of subject matter differences in instruction: Analysis of teacher's guides, textbooks, and methods books.* Final report to the Spencer Foundation. Chicago: University of Chicago.

Stodolsky, S. S., T. L. Ferguson, and K. Wimpelberg. 1981. The recitation persists, but what does it look like? *Journal of Curriculum Studies* 13, no. 2:121–30.

Superka, D. P., S. Hawke, and I. Morrissett. 1980. The current and future status of social studies. *Social Education* 44:362–69.

Suydam, M. N., and A. Osborne. 1977. *The status of pre-college science, mathematics, and social studies education: 1955–1975.* Vol. 2, *Mathematics education.* SE 78-73, vol. 2, National Science Foundation contract no. C 7620627. Washington, D.C.: U.S. Government Printing Office.

Thomas, J. A., and F. Kemmerer. 1983. *Money, time and learning.* Final report, National Institute of Education contract no. 400-77-0094. Chicago: University of Chicago. ERIC no. ED242 096.

Tobias, S. 1982. When do instructional methods make a difference? *Educational Researcher* 11, no. 4:4–9.

Travers, K. J., L. Pikaart, M. N. Suydam, and G. E. Runion. 1977. *Mathematics teaching.* New York: Harper and Row.

University of Chicago School Mathematics Project (UCSMP). 1984. Evaluation report on the elementary component. University of Chicago. Typescript.

Usiskin, Z., J. Flanders, C. Hynes, L. Polonsky, S. Porter, and S. Viktora. 1986. *Transition mathematics*. Chicago: University of Chicago School Mathematics Project.

Walker, D. 1976. *The IEA six subject survey: An empirical study of education in twenty-one countries*. New York: Wiley.

Weiss, I. 1978. *Report of the 1977 National Survey of Science, Mathematics and Social Studies Education*. Research Triangle Park, N.C.: Research Triangle Institute.

Westbury, I. 1978. Research into classroom processes: A review of ten years' work. *Curriculum Studies* 10, no. 4:283–308.

Wittrock, M. C. 1986. Students' thought processes. In *Handbook of research on teaching*, 3d ed., ed. M. C. Wittrock. New York: Macmillan.

Wright, H. F. 1967. *Recording and analyzing child behavior with ecological data from an American town*. New York: Harper and Row.

Index

Accountability, 4–5, 108–10
Achievement tests, 4–5, 76, 77, 96–97, 108–9, 131
Activity segments: data coding of, 26–30; defined, 11–12; description of, 35–62; durations of, 171–73; number of, 170; patterns of, 62–66; properties of, 12–15; simultaneous, 61–62
Activity structures: and accountability, 108–10; community influences on, 105–6; and content/topics, 115–17; defined, 11–12; observation of, 22–26; and student characteristics, 107–8; and teacher preferences/values, 113–15; and textbooks, 110–13
Adams, R. S., 104
Ahlbrand, W. P., 91
Airasian, P. W., 118
Alleman-Brooks, J., 118
Amarel, M., 113
Anderson, L. M., 118
Anderson, L. W., 15
Anthropology, 8, 34, 115, 118
Arithmetic, 7–8
Arlin, M., 11
Armbruster, B. B., 113, 123, 180n.1
Art, 104
Attitudes, student, toward subject matter, 124–29. See also Student involvement
Audiovisual pacing. See Mechanical pacing

"Back-to-basics" movement, 106
Barker, R. G., 11

Barr, R., 107, 177n.3
Basic subjects, 7, 15, 104; and accountability, 4–5, 108–9; concept of, 4–5; and student involvement, 18, 19, 83, 94; time allocation in, 5, 57
Bell, J., 7
Bell, M., 7
Belli, G., 110, 111, 115
Berger, P. L., 117
Berliner, D. C., 76, 76, 84, 177n.1
Biber, B., 120
Biddle, B., 97, 104
Bloom, B. S., 14, 59–60, 81, 82, 98, 101, 148
Blumenfeld, P. C., 113, 118, 120
Breer, P. E., 117
Brophy, J. E., 93–94, 97
Brubaker, N. L., 118
Brush, L. R., 126–27
Burns, R. B., 12
Buros, O. K., 108–9
Bussis, A. M., 113

Cahen, L. S., 76, 84
Career education, 9, 106
Carey, S., 116
Carpenter, T. P., 7, 123–24, 126, 128
Center for the Study of Instruction (CSI), 10
Chall, J., 3
Checking work, 17, 60; coding criteria for, 27, 144–45; in program variants, 66–67, 69; in sample segments, 35, 41–43; and segment patterns, 63; and student involvement, 87–91, 95; value of, 99

Child pacing, 13, 14; coding criteria for, 147; and cognitive level, 79, 100; in sample segments, 49, 53, 63, 66, 70; and student involvement, 13, 18–19, 84–86
Child-child pacing. *See* Cooperative pacing
China, mathematics instruction in, 116
Chitenden, E. A., 113
Church, R. L., 76
Civics, 8, 34
Clark, C. M., 12, 110, 115
Class composition, 107–8
Cognitive level: coding criteria for, 26–27, 148–53; defined, 13–15; and direct instruction model, 17, 77; in group-work programs, 69, 79, 81, 115, 134; and individual teacher consistency, 70, 72, 73; and pacing, 78–82, 98–101; in sample segments, 58–60, 78–79; and segment patterns, 62–66; and student involvement, 16–17, 82–95, 134; and teachers' manuals, 112
Cohen, E. G., 132
Community influences on instruction, 105–6
Cooperative pacing, 13, 14; coding criteria for, 147; and cognitive level, 79, 81; in sample segments, 49, 53; and student involvement, 84–86, 94, 95. *See also* Peer work groups
Corbitt, M. K., 123–24
Creativity, 78, 120
Cuban, L., 76, 95
Curriculum: implicit, 117; as instructional activity determinant, 115–17; mathematics, 7–8, 31–34; social studies, 8–11, 34–35. *See also* Subject matter

Davidson, N., 109
Demonstrations, 12–13, 43; coding criteria for, 144
Dewey, J., 14, 109
Direct instruction model, 17, 18, 76–78, 134
Discussion, 42; coding criteria for, 143
Dishaw, M. M., 76, 84

Doyle, W., 118, 120
Dreeben, R., 107, 117, 177n.3
Duffy, G. G., 118
Dunkin, M., 97
Durkin, D., 110

Easley, J., 7, 104, 123
Eastern Europe, mathematics instruction in, 7
Economics, 8, 34
Education Development Center, 10
Elbaz, F., 115
Ellis, A. K., 6, 9
Engelhart, M. D., 14, 59–60, 81, 82, 98, 101, 148
English, instruction in, 126, 127
Enrichment subjects, 7, 15, 104; and accountability, 4–5, 109; concept of, 4–5; and student involvement, 18, 19, 83, 94, 98; time allocation in, 57
Erickson, F., 118
Evertson, C. M., 130
Existential fallacy, 129–31
Expanding environment principle, 9

Feedback: from checking work, 99; coding criteria for, 26–27, 159–65; defined, 159; and direct instruction model, 77; and student involvement, 13
Feiman-Nemser, S., 114
Ferguson, T. L., 91–92, 107
Fey, J. T., 7, 123
Filby, N. N., 76, 84
Fisher, L. W., 84
Flanders, J., 7, 113
Floden, R., 110, 111, 115, 180n.13
Foreign languages, 126–28
Freeman, D. J., 110, 111, 115, 180n.13
Freeman, F. N., 6
Furst, E. J., 14, 59–60, 81, 82, 98, 101, 148
Fuson, K. C., 116

Gage, N. L., 97, 130
Gall, M. D., 92
Geography, 8, 9, 34, 35, 69, 115–16
Geometry, 7, 8, 34, 119
Giaconia, R. M., 120

Glaessner, B. E., 125
Goffman, E., 117
Good, T. L., 93–94, 97, 99
Goodlad, J. I., 19, 78, 97, 104, 105, 111, 123, 126, 128
Grade level: and instructional pattern, 104–5; and student attitudes toward subjects, 126–27
Grades, 120
Grannis, J. C., 12, 13, 18, 19, 58, 77, 94, 116, 147
Graybeal, S. S., 6, 53, 69, 100, 109, 111, 179n.8
Green, J. L., 130
Greeno, J. G., 119
Grouws, D. A., 99
Gump, P. V., 11, 12, 13, 16, 26, 61, 66, 77, 84, 147

Ham, M., 116
Haney, W., 108
Hare, P., 109, 132
Hawke, S., 10
Hawkins, D., 13–14
Hedges, L. V., 120
Hertz-Lazarowitz, R., 109, 132
Hill, W. H., 14, 59–60, 81, 82, 98, 101, 148
History, 8, 9, 34, 35, 69, 115–16, 119
Hoetker, A. J., 91
Homework, 85, 99, 106
Horwitz, R. A., 3–4, 120
Hoyles, C., 125
Husen, T., 116
Hynes, C., 113

Instruction: direct model of, 17, 18, 76–78, 134; existential fallacy in, 129–31; individualized, in mathematics, 67–68, 73–74, 105–6, 129, 130; intellectual quality of, 78, 97–98, 135; progressive, 109–10, 115; school philosophy of, 106–7; and subject matter, 3–11; teacher-centered versus student-centered, 56–57, 66–69, 76. See also Learning
Instructional format: coding criteria for, 26–27, 142–47; defined, 12–13, 142; and individual teacher con-

sistency, 70–73; in sample segments, 40–44; and segment patterns, 62–66; and teachers' manuals, 112

Jackson, E., 12
Jackson, P. W., 97, 117
Japan, mathematics instruction in, 7, 116
Jarolimek, J., 9–10, 35
Jones, L. V., 7

Kagan, J., 175n.2
Kaskowitz, D., 76, 94
Kellaghan, T., 118
Kemmerer, F., 105–6, 176n.4, 179n.11
Kepner, H. S., 123–24
Kim, M. S., 116
Kluckhohn, C., 117
Knappen, L., 110, 111, 115, 180n.13
Kounin, J. S., 16
Krammer, H. P., 110
Krathwohl, D. R., 14, 59–60, 81, 82, 98, 101, 148
Kuhs, T., 110, 111, 115, 180n.13

Learning: meaning of, 117–29; routes to, 121–26; student involvement in process of, 95–96. See also Instruction
Leavey, M., 109
Lectures, 41, 42, 105; coding criteria for, 143–44
Lee, S., 116, 128
Leinhardt, G., 114
Lindquist, M. M., 123–24
Locke, E. A., 117
Luchins, A. S., 118
Lucker, G. W., 116, 128

Luckmann, T., 117

MACOS. See Man: A Course of Study
Madaus, G. F., 118
Madden, N. A., 109
Man: A Course of Study (MACOS), 10, 34, 69, 89–90, 100, 106
Man and His World, 10
Marliave, R. S., 76, 84

Marshall, H., 99
Marton, F., 117
Materials, 48–49, 58, 70. *See also* Textbooks
Mathematics instruction, 1–2; and accountability, 4, 5, 109; community influences on, 105–6; curriculum and content in, 7–8, 115–16; and direct instruction model, 76, 77; form of, 3–7; learning process in, 119, 122–25; student attitudes toward, 124–29; and teacher preferences/values, 114; textbooks as determinants of, 110–13, 122
Mathematics instruction, in sample classrooms: earlier study results compared with results on, 97–102; generalizability of findings from, 104–5; instructional activity in, 35, 41–62; learning environment organization in, 76–82; program variants in, 66–68, 115; research methods used with, 20–30; segment patterns in, 62–66; and student involvement, 82–97, 131, 134; topics in, 31–34
Mead, G. H., 117
Mechanical pacing, 13, 14; coding criteria for, 147; in sample segments, 49, 70–71, 79
Meece, J., 120
Mergendoller, J., 113, 118
Minuchin, P., 120
Missouri Mathematics Program, 99
Moore, J. E., 76, 84
Morrissett, I., 9–10
Mosenthal, J., 113, 180n.1
Music, 104

National Advisory Committee on Mathematical Education, 122–23
National Assessment of Educational Progress, 126
Netherlands, mathematics instruction in, 110
"New math," 8
"New social studies," 9–10
Nicely, R. F., Jr., 112

Occupancy time distributions, defined, 40–41
Options. *See* Student options
Orlandi, L. R., 9, 14, 59, 148
Osborne, A., 104
Ozcelik, D. A., 175n.1

Pacing: coding criteria for, 26–27, 147; and cognitive level, 78–82, 98–101; defined, 13–14, 147; and direct instruction model, 77; individual teacher consistency in, 70–71, 73; in sample segments, 40, 49–56, 78–79; and segment patterns, 62–66; and student involvement, 13, 18–19, 82–95. *See also* Child pacing; Cooperative pacing; Mechanical pacing; Teacher pacing
Peer work groups, 12–13; and cognitive level, 69, 79, 81, 115, 134; defined, 53; goals of, 132–33; and learning process, 118, 119, 129; in sample classes, 68–69; and student involvement, 84–86. *See also* Cooperative pacing
Perrone, V., 179n.13
Peterson, P. L., 115
Pintrich, P. R., 120
Pipho, C., 106
Plihal, J. E., 113
Polonsky, L., 113
Porter, A. C., 110, 111, 115, 180n.13
Porter, S., 113
Posner, G., 113, 118
Preparatory segments, 17, 42; student responses to, 89–90, 95, 98–100
Progressive education movement, 109–10, 115
Psychology, 34, 115
Public opinion, 106

Raizen, S. A., 7
Reading, 107, 110; activity segments in, 11–12; as basic subject, 4–5; and direct instruction model, 76, 77, 134; methods of instruction in, 3

Recitation, 12, 13, 118, 130; coding criteria for, 27–28, 143; in high school, 105 in program variants, 66–67, 69; in sample segments, 35, 41–44, 98; and segment patterns, 63, 66; and student involvement, 87–89, 91–94, 96, 100; and teachers' manuals, 111, 112
Research skills, 101, 124, 133
Reys, R. E., 123–24
Romberg, T. A., 7
Rosenholtz, S. J., 120
Rosenshine, B. V., 14, 15, 18, 76–78, 93–94
Ross, R. P., 11
Runes, D. D., 180n.4

Saljo, R., 117
Salomon, G., 118
Schmidt, W., 110, 111, 115, 180n.13
Schoenfeld, A. H., 119
Schwille, J., 110, 111, 115, 180n.13
Science instruction, 5, 126–28
Seatwork, 12, 13, 118; coding criteria for, 27, 142–43; in program variants, 66–67, 69; in sample segments, 35, 41–44, 97–98; and segment patterns, 63; and student involvement, 13, 15, 18, 84–85; student options in, 56–57; and teachers' manuals, 111
Sedlak, M. W., 76
Segment distributions, defined, 40–41
Shapiro, E., 120
Sharan, S., 109, 132
Shavelson, R. J., 115
Shulman, L. S., 114, 118
Silver, E. A., 3
Sirotnik, K. A., 97
Slavin, R. E., 14, 100, 109, 119, 129
Soar, R. M., 76
Soar, R. S., 76
Social sciences: educational research in, 130; on learning, 118
Social studies instruction, 1–2; and accountability, 4, 5, 109; community influences on, 106; curriculum and

content in, 8–11, 115–16; form of, 3–7; learning process in, 118, 122–24; student attitudes toward, 126–29; and teacher preferences/values, 113; textbooks as determinants of, 111–13, 122
Social studies instruction, in sample classrooms: earlier study results compared with results on, 97–102; generalizability of findings from, 104–5; instructional activity in, 35–62; learning environment organization in, 76–82; program variants in, 68–70, 115; research methods used with, 20–30; segment patterns in, 62–66; and student involvement, 82–97, 131, 134; topics in, 31–34
Socioeconomic status (SES), 20, 22, 30, 94, 105–7
Sociology, 8, 115
Soviet Union, mathematics instruction in, 116
Squire, J. R., 112
Stake, R. E., 7, 104, 123
Stallings, J., 13, 76, 94
Stano, S. A., 92
Stern, P., 115
Stevenson, H., 116, 128
Stigler, J. W., 116, 128
Stodolsky, S. S., 6, 15, 19, 53, 69, 72, 91–92, 100, 109, 111, 114, 119, 124–25, 132, 133, 176nn.9,1, 179n.8
Student behavior patterns: coding criteria for, 26–27, 153–59; defined, 13; and individual teacher consistency, 70; in sample segments, 44–48; and segment patterns, 62–66
Student interaction, and student involvement, 13
Student interaction, expected: coding criteria for, 26–27, 165–66; in sample segments, 49–56; and segment patterns, 62–66
Student involvement, 2–3, 13, 21; coding criteria for, 28, 168; and cognitive level, 16–17, 82–95, 134;

Student involvement, *cont.*
concept of, 15–19; and direct instruction model, 77–78, 93–94; in
learning process, 95–96; and pacing, 78–82, 98–101; and teacher
consistency, 70; and teacher prefer-
ences/values, 113
Student location: coding criteria for, 26–
27, 167–68; in sample segments, 57
Student options, 109–10; coding criteria
for, 26–27, 166–67; defined, 166; in
sample segments, 56–57; and student involvement, 13
Students: characteristics of, and instructional differentiation, 107–8;
selection of, for samples, 20–26;
subject matter attitudes of, 124–29
Subject matter: and form of instruction,
3–11; generalizability of study findings with respect to, 104–5; importance of, 1–3; student attitudes
toward, 124–29
Superka, D. P., 10
Suydam, M. N., 104
Swarthout, D., 113, 118

Taxonomy of Educational Objectives
(Bloom et al.), 14, 59–60, 81, 82,
98, 101, 148
Teacher pacing, 13, 14; coding criteria
for, 147; and cognitive level, 79–82,
99; in sample segments, 49, 53, 63–
66, 70, 97–98; and student involvement, 18, 84–93, 95, 97–101
Teachers: consistency of individual, 70–
73, 131–32; educational studies
centered on, 97; evaluation of, 133–
34; and feedback, 56–57; and
group-work activities, 53, 95, 132–
33; instructional activity choices by,
131–36; leadership roles of, 26–27,
61–63; observations of, in sample
classrooms, 20–26; preferences and

values of, and instructional activity,
113–15; and routes to learning,
122–24; and teacher-centered approaches, 56–57, 66–69, 76
Teachers' manuals, 110–12
Testing: achievement, 4–5, 76, 77, 96–
97, 108–9, 131; and learning concept of students, 118; pattern of, in
samples, 63, 66–67
Textbooks, 67, 72, 74, 89; feedback
from, 58; and instructional differentiation, 106, 110–13, 116; in
mathematics curriculum, 7, 8; as
route to learning, 122–25; used in
sample classes, 48–49
Thomas, J. A., 105–6, 176n.4, 179n.11
Time allocation: in sample segments,
57; and subject matter, 4–5
Tobias, S., 119
Transitions, 11; number and duration
of, 30

University of Chicago School Mathematics Project, 104
Usiskin, Z., 113

Viktora, S., 113

Walker, D., 116
Webb, C. D., 109, 132
Weinstein, R., 99
Weiss, I., 5, 10, 57, 104
Wessels, K., 120
Westbury, I., 104
Wilson, B., 120
Wimpelberg, K., 91–92
Wittrock, M. C., 175n.1
Work groups. *See* Peer work groups
Wright, H. F., 53–56

Yinger, R. J., 12, 110, 115

Zimiles, H., 120

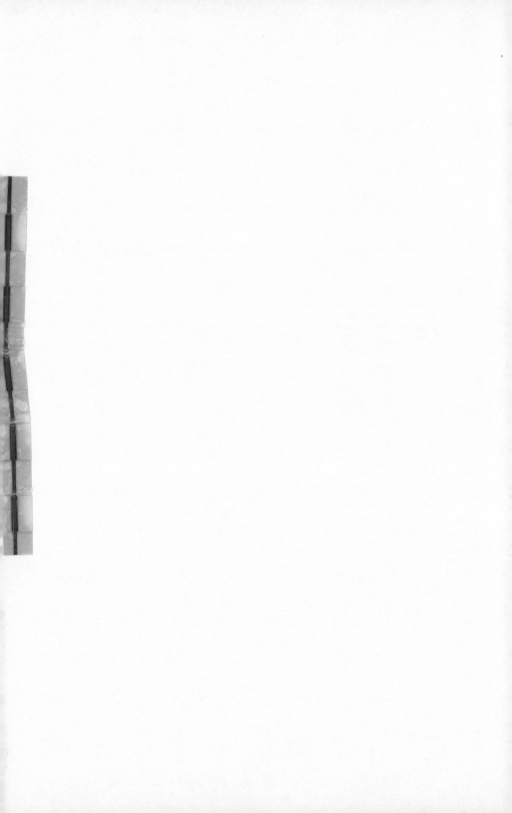

23,45

371.11
St 63
1988

122679